CONTEMPORARY WORLD THEOLOGY

A Layman's Guidebook

By
**HARVIE
M.
CONN**

PRESBYTERIAN AND REFORMED PUBLISHING CO.
Box 817
Phillipsburg, New Jersey 08865

To
Dorothy

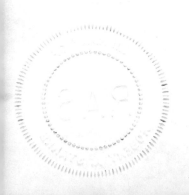

TABLE OF CONTENTS

PREFACE

The ecumenical movement reminds us repeatedly that the Christian is divided into too many classifications—Catholic, Presbyterian, Methodist, Baptist, Episcopalian. It also attempts to remind us that these divisions are relatively meaningless.

This book is, in some sense, the history of such divisions. But, as one can quickly see, it does not concentrate on denominations but on doctrine. And its central thrust is that the greatest divisions within the Christian church are not those that separate Presbyterians and Methodists, Baptists and Episcopalians, what many have come to call "denominationalism." The greatest division is between those who believe the self-authenticating Christ of the Bible and those who do not, between those who proclaim a sovereign, triune God, self-authenticating and self-revealing, and those who do not, between those who, in simple faith, believe that the world is a battleground of supernatural forces and those who do not.

This division is not relatively meaningless. As the famed Presbyterian scholar, J. Gresham Machen, once claimed, it is the division that separates, not one form of Christianity from another form of Christianity, but one religion from another religion, Christianity from what Machen reluctantly called "liberalism" (though "naturalism" he felt to be a better descriptive term).

The crucial issue in this division is not politics or the graciousness with which one debates issues in the courts of the church. The crucial issue is also not even our personal relationship to Jesus Christ. To be sure, the decision regarding Jesus Christ divides Christian from non-Christian, a believer in Jesus from a believer in Confucius. But our question is theology, not personal faith. And the crucial issue that divides sound teaching and good theology from false teaching and bad theology is the authority of Scripture. Shall we believe the Bible or shall we not?

In making the trustworthiness of the Bible the touchstone of our appraisal of theology, we must issue a warning. We do not judge individuals' saving relationships to Jesus Christ in our study. As Harold O. J. Brown has put it, "There are many theological 'liberals' who are really true Christians, because Christianity in the individual depends on the attitude of the heart toward Jesus Christ, and this is not always consistent with one's theology or one's morals. There are Christians who offer bad examples of theology, just as there are Christians who offer bad examples of morality. . . . The Christian who wishes to preserve both his sanity and his charity in dealing with theological liberals and radicals must keep both facts in mind: first, a Christian may have a low (liberal) theology and/or a low (permissive, hedonistic, relativistic) morality, and still remain a Christian: second, no low theology is Christian theology and no low morality is Christian morality. A believing Christian with either a low theology or a low morality is in for trouble in his own life and will cause trouble in the lives of others. . . ."[1]

It is in the light of the liberal/naturalistic-Christian chasm that we criticise. We use terms such as "Reformed," "Calvinistic," to describe the perspective from which we offer our criticism. We agree with Bultmann that "exegesis without presuppositions is impossible."[2] But, unlike Bultmann,

---

1. Harold O. J. Brown, *The Protest of a Troubled Protestant* (New Rochelle, N. Y.: Arlington House, 1969), p. 134.
2. Rudolf Bultmann, *Existence and Faith* (New York: Living Age Books, 1960), pp. 289 ff.

whose presuppositions are existentialist, we declare ours to be those which the Bible itself provides us. We move from the Scriptures, through the Scriptures, to the Scriptures. Many will condemn this kind of criticism as arguing in a circle, or debating within a closed system. Our only rebuttal is that all arguing, as even Bultmann has conceded, is arguing in a circle.[3] The only question becomes, Who has drawn the circle? Who has closed the system? Insofar as the circle is a Bible-centered one, it is also God-centered. And a God-centered mind is always closed, in the most beautiful sense. Our appeal is for more closed minds, more arguing in terms of God's circle.

The most obvious thrust of this handbook is critical. But it is not at all intended to be detailed either as an introduction to contemporary world theology or as an analysis. As its title intimates, it offers a sketch, a skeletal outline, a guidebook to streets and places of interest. At the same time, like any guidebook, it is concerned to give the widest picture possible. And so we seek not only to put our finger on the main movements but to be sure that these movements are seen as a system and not a conglomeration of street lights and road signs. Our criticism is also concerned, not so much with road signs, as with systems. With that deliberate purpose in mind, we commend strongly the writings of Dr. Cornelius Van Til as the work of a man who is concerned with systems-criticism and with underlying presuppositions.

It is in Dr. Van Til's structuring of today's theological problems that this work basically stands. But we write for laymen to whom this theological world seems a new country. And for anyone travelling in new countries, guidebooks are more profitable at first than 600-page textbooks. We write also with the lands of the so-called "younger churches"

---

3. For a full defense of circular reasoning, consult Cornelius Van Til, *The Defense of the Faith* (Philadelphia: Presbyterian and Reformed Publishing Co., 1967), pp. 99 ff., 179 ff.

in mind, with pastors in mind whose most advanced theological training may not reach beyond a Bible institute or a program of theological education by extension, but who are troubled by the voices they hear which do not seem to ring with a biblical note. It is our hope that this handbook may serve them in some small way as well. Contemporary theology is too truly "world theology" to forget the global village in which we all live.

For this reason, the Western reader will quickly notice the many references to an Asian, and particularly a Korean, setting. They are designed to indicate the width of theological formulations today, and they indicate also the origins of these studies. The guidebook was originally prepared for the Korean Christian weekly newspaper, the *Christian Times*, and for its lay reader. The author has felt that by retaining the original and more local materials, it will be easier to remember the work's beginnings and its thrust.

With some pressure, the author resists the temptation to publish this title under his Korean name. Though not himself a native-born Korean, he has written originally for the Korean church, in a Korean context, subject to all the limitations of available resource material and time that make the preaching of the gospel in Korea an adventure and, at the same time, a frustration. It was encouraged by Korean Christians, corrected and prodded by them. Yet it also has benefited beyond words from the kind and most helpful criticism of the author's teaching master, Dr. Cornelius Van Til. He has taken much time to guide the ramblings of one of his more foolish disciples. The Rev. John J. Mitchell, editor of *The Presbyterian Guardian*, also has taken his own time to read this work and offer his needed advice. Thus, in the end, it represents a Korean-American project, in the best traditions of the apostle Paul (Gal. 3:28).

In that spirit, our pen wishes to sign the work as Kan Ha-bae, but our publisher insists that Harvie M. Conn may be easier to pronounce.

CHAPTER I

BEFORE 1919

Contemporary theology, in a real sense, was born in the study of a church in Switzerland, about sixteen miles south of the German border. The inaugurator was a young pastor, Karl Barth (1886–1968), who had gone there in 1911, at the age of 25. And the manifesto of this new theological turning-point in history, the initial announcement of a new theological era, came in the form of Barth's commentary on Romans in 1919. What the general significance of that book meant will be sketched in the next chapter of our study.

In this opening chapter, we are seeking only to show that even the shifts of theological currents since 1919 are part of a larger ocean, and that the difference between "modern" theology and "contemporary" theology is sometimes less a difference and more an emphasis building upon common presuppositions. Even what has so often been referred to as Barth's dropping a bombshell in the playground of the theologians may be more accurately described as a cannonade on one part of the playground from another part of the same playground. In that sense, Barth's so-called "Copernican revolution" began not in 1919 but 200 years before, in the study of the philosopher-prince of the Enlightenment, Immanuel Kant (1724–1804).[1]

---

1. Cornelius Van Til, *The Reformed Pastor and Modern Thought* (Nutley, N. J.: Presbyterian and Reformed Publishing Co., 1971), pp. 106-131.

The idea of the world coming of age did not originate with Dietrich Bonhoeffer. It was the theme song of the Renaissance and of the Western Enlightenment era, an era that has left its permanent stamp on everything modern. Kant systematized "modern man's confidence in the power of reason to grapple with material things and its incompetence to deal with anything beyond."[2] And in doing so, he cast a shadow not merely over the nineteenth century but over the twentieth century as well. In 1784, Kant summed up the demands of new Enlightenment when he defined it as man's emergence from his self-inflicted immaturity. This immaturity is found in man's reliance upon any authority external to himself. Enlightenment and autonomy become identical, and modern man's motto becomes "Dare to use your own understanding," "Freedom to think without sanctions, without direction external to man himself," "Awakening from dogmatic slumber."[3]

The Christian senses a familiar ring of antiquity to this supposedly new sound. Satan had also questioned any authority external to man himself in the garden of Eden. "Indeed, has God said?" he had asked (Gen. 3:1). He also invited man to pursue his own free path of Enlightenment. "God knows," he reminded Eve, "that in the day you eat from it your eyes will be opened and you will be like God, knowing good and evil" (Gen. 3:5). But, with Kant and the Enlightenment spirit of the modern age, there had come some new twists to an old angle.

1. There was, and is, a new set of religious presuppositions that mold modern man's thought. Man, as the image of God, is always building categories by which he can view himself, God, and the world. From what the Bible calls

---

2. Colin Brown, *Philosophy and the Christian Faith* (Chicago: Inter-Varsity Press, 1969), p. 91.

3. Immanuel Kant, "Beantwortung der Frage: Was ist Aufklarung?," *Berlinische Monatsschrift*, December, 1784, (*Gesammelte Schriften*, Berlin, VIII, p. 35).

man's "heart," from everything that makes him man, from the center that relates him everywhere and always to God, "from it flow the springs of life" (Prov. 4:23). "For as he thinketh in his heart, so is he" (Prov. 23:7).

The "heart" of the ancient Greek world had built its religious ground rules around the contradictions of form and matter.[4] In the Middle Ages, the West had accommodated those basically non-Christian, covenant-breaking ideas to a new compromise with Christian principles and come up with another set framed around the ideas of nature and grace. Neither religious theme of nature or grace represented purely biblical ground rules for self-understanding. The presupposition of nature was not the biblical concept of a created world in subjection to its Creator. It was an autonomous sub-structure that put the old Greek ideas of form—matter in a new dress, modified by new demands. In this compromise, grace also lost its distinctively Christian character, and became more a perfecting form of superstructure rather than a radical act of transformation by the sovereign God. The Middle Ages synthesis of Thomas Aquinas had emancipated natural man from supernatural grace.

Kant and the Enlightenment spirit now made that emancipation more than merely accommodation. For the first time in Western civilization, nature and grace were severed in a consistent, developed, self-conscious form. Grace disappeared in the religious thinking of modern man and its place was taken by the category of freedom. Man was to be reborn as a completely free and autonomous personality and released from all controls over his thinking. And, in this spirit, even the category of nature, still retained from the medieval synthesis, was transformed. Nature became a "macrocosmic sphere within which human personality

---

4. For a simple explanation of these religious antinomies, consult Cornelius Van Til, *The Great Debate Today* (Nutley, N. J.: Presbyterian and Reformed Publishing Co., 1971), pp. 179-188.

could exercise its autonomy. Nature was interpreted as an infinite field to be controlled by autonomous mathematical thought."[5]

The history of Western thought and Western theology since Kant is the history of how these religious presuppositions, building on borrowed Christian capital and therefore self-contradictory, mold a new world.

2. There was, and is, a more consistently developed sense of man-centered autonomy. The Enlightenment "heart" had called for an emancipated human freedom, an autonomous nature where fact was severed from its meaning in God, and therefore brutalized. This religious attitude produced a quite high assessment of all of man's capacities, and especially of human reason as the final authority, the ultimate criterion for truth. Reason and reason alone becomes adequate for judging the world of the phenomenon and the world of the noumenon.[6]

For Kant this autonomy meant the replacing of the Christian concept of "autonomous" revelation, of the self-authenticating God revealing himself through the Bible, by man's autonomous reason. In the ultimate sense, it is "universal human reason" which Kant labels as "the su-

---

5. Vincent Brummer, *Transcendental Criticism and Christian Philosophy* (Franeker: T. Wever, 1961), p. 98. A fuller explanation of these themes will be found in Herman Dooyeweerd, *In the Twilight of Western Thought* (Philadelphia: Presbyterian and Reformed Publishing Co., 1960).
6. It is a most unfortunate feature of the work of the Calvinistic critic, Francis Schaeffer, that, though helpful in so many areas, he cannot fully see the radical influence of man's religious presuppositions on his use of the reason nor the inadequacy of the reason as an ultimate judge. Compare *The God Who Is There* (Chicago: Inter-Varsity Press, 1968), pp. 108 ff. As others have well seen, Schaeffer's whole presentation is oriented "around the assumption that man must decide for himself whether God's written revelation is true" (John J. Mitchell, "A Critique of F. A. Schaeffer's *The God Who Is There*," unpublished paper read before the Student Association of Westminster Theological Seminary, February, 1969, p. 5).

premely commanding principle."[7] "True religion is to consist not in the knowing or considering of what God does or has done for our salvation but in what we must do to become worthy of it . . . and of its necessity every man can become wholly certain without any Scriptural learning whatever."[8]

It is not far from this concept of rational autonomy to Bultmann's concept of demythologization, where modern man must create new myths to authenticate the Bible's demands for self-understanding. Nor is it very far from autonomous reason as judge over revelation to Pannenberg's rational analysis of the resurrection narratives as permeated with legends, or Cullmann's refusal to credit the Genesis records of creation as authentic, rationally credible history.

3. There was, and is, a more consistently developed relativism. David Hume, the Scottish philosopher (1711–1776), had formulated for the Enlightenment world the problem of knowledge. His skepticism had questioned whether anyone could prove the existence of anything, either outside oneself or even oneself. Cause and effect, God as Origin, man as originated—all are equally elusive. We have the data of our senses, but nothing beyond that.

Kant took from Hume the problem of knowledge and "gave it back as if it were the solution."[9] He created two worlds—the world of the phenomena and the world of the noumena, the world perceived by reason through the raw material of the senses, and the world of God, freedom and immortality, regulative ideas which cannot be perceived by reason but must have their place in our lives as if they were real objects knowable by reason.

The effect of all of this was, and is, devastating. God is strait-jacketed by Kant into a sound-proof bulkhead, tied to the phenomenal world only by Kant's umbilical cord of

---

7. Immanuel Kant, *Religion Within the Limits of Reason Alone* (Chicago: Open Court Publishing Co., c. 1934), p. 152.

8. *Ibid.*, p. 123.

9. C. Brown, *op. cit.*, p. 96.

5

man's need for the idea of God in the world of ethics. The door is not closed altogether on God, but it is so small that there is no room for the sovereign God "whose train fills the temple" (Isa. 6:1) to squeeze through. Similarly, since man cannot actually perceive things as they are in themselves (whether in the phenomenal or the noumenal world), he cannot squeeze through that door to know God. God has been effectively isolated from man and man has been effectively isolated from God.

This isolation of God into the noumenal world is a favorite theme of contemporary theology. It is reinforced by existentialism's increased emphasis on freedom, and appears, in modified form, in Barth's early writing on God as "the wholly Other," as the one who "cannot be explained, as an object can." It reproduces itself in the neo-orthodox division between *Historie* and *Geschichte*, in Bultmann's distinctions between "the historical Jesus" and "the kerygmatic Christ," or, to use Kant's language, the phenomenal Jesus and the noumenal Christ. Its relativism regarding the divine origin of revelation leads to a new stress on the "humanity" of the Bible, and a new Barthian definition of revelation itself as "the divine-human encounter," the noumenal touching the phenomenal but not entering. It produces in Moltmann a "theology of hope," completely skeptical about any eschatological end to phenomenal history, yet still able to speak of a noumenal future.

4. There was, and is, the establishment of the so-called historical-critical method. The Enlightenment had called for autonomy from any traditional sets of Christian belief. It also called for a critical methodology that would also be fully consistent with this self-conscious autonomy. In the investigation of the past, the historian must also be autonomous. Even with regard to the biblical documents, this autonomy must be strictly preserved.

This autonomy of method over against biblical text makes certain assumptions still ruthlessly guarded by the historical-

6

critical method.[10] It means an abandonment of the doctrine of verbal inspiration. The deistic concept of nature and God which was part of the spawning process of the Enlightenment found no place for a divine intervention of God into creation through any supernatural, revelatory manner. German idealism follows this non-intervention policy most severely. It means also the introduction of distinction and discontinuity between the Word of God on the one hand and the Bible on the other. And coupled with this is the methodological presumption that there are errors in the Bible. As the proper object of historical method, the Bible is to be treated like any other set of documents from the past. And like any other document, it is subject to the intrusion of error.

This approach to the Bible remains today one of the distinguishing features of naturalistic criticism, whether in its more conservative form (as exemplified by men like Oscar Cullmann and Wolfhart Pannenberg) or in its more radical expressions (among men like Tillich, John Robinson, and the secular theologians). Barth and Bultmann, despite all the internecine debate, remain at one in their retention of this methodology. The sharp debates heard between contemporary naturalistic theologians today—and one should not under-emphasize their sharpness—are still carried on within basically the same methodological framework which the Enlightenment has left us as their heritage.[11]

5. The result of this methodology was, and is, a radical separation between history and faith. G. E. Lessing (1729–

---

10. I am most indebted to Dr. Richard B. Gaffin of Westminster Theological Seminary for drawing the attention of his students to the following material during class sessions in the fall of 1971.

11. The usefulness of the historical-critical method seems to be becoming popular even in hitherto Reformed circles in the Netherlands. Note the cogent criticism of what seems to be a recognition of the validity of its presuppositions in G. C. Berkouwer's new attitudes as cited by C. Van Til, *The Sovereignty of Grace* (Nutley, N. J.: Presbyterian and Reformed Publishing Co., 1969).

1781) had formulated that separation during the Enlightenment times as an "ugly, broad ditch" which he himself said he was incapable of jumping. But such a leap, Lessing also said, was unnecessary. The truth of religion and of rational Christianity does not depend upon the accidents of history's truths but upon the truth of its teaching.[12] The true worth of any religion does not depend on history, he said, but on its capacity to transform life through love.

Lessing's famous parable of the three rings emphasizes this disjunction sharply. Brown has summarized it this way: "There was once an ancient ring which had the power to bestow upon its owner the gift of being loved by God and man. This was passed on down many generations until it came into the possession of a father who had three sons equally dear to him. To resolve the dilemma, he had two replicas made and gave a ring to each son. After his death all three claimed to possess the true ring. But, as with religion, the original cannot be traced. Historical investigation is of no avail. But a wise judge counsels each son to behave as if he had the true ring and prove it by deeds of love. Thus in the end it will not matter who had the original. The three sons represent Judaism, Christianity and Islam. One day they will transcend themselves and become united in a universal religion of love."[13]

Repeatedly in the chapters that follow, this disjunction between history and faith will be recognized and repeatedly, in the same manner as Lessing, the modern theologian will say that though the recorded history of Christianity may not be accepted to greater or lesser degree, the teaching of Christianity may be accepted to greater or lesser degree. Barth will retain it as he discards the question of whether the snake in the garden of Eden spoke as of lesser importance than what the snake said. Bultmann will retain

12. G. E. Lessing, *Theological Writings* (London: Adam and Charles Black, 1956), pp. 51-56.
13. C. Brown, *op. cit.*, p. 89.

it as he repudiates the gospel records as historically dubious productions on the one hand, and embraces them for their existential understanding of the self, on the other hand. Moltmann will retain it as he scorns the classic Christian notion of eschatology as the church waiting for the future of the risen Lord in history and yet speaks of the church oriented to the future. John Robinson will retain it as he rejects the idea of heaven as a "place up there" and yet insists on a new dimension to life as "being in depth" and God as "the ground of being."

CHAPTER II

1919 AND AFTER

In 1919, the pastor of a small church in Switzerland published a commentary so radical in its scope that one writer has said Karl Barth took a letter written in first century Greek and made it a special delivery to twentieth century man. A Catholic theologian speaks of this commentary on Romans as a Copernican revolution in Protestant theology which put an end to the dominance of liberal thought. Another called the book "a bombshell on the playground of the theologians."[1]

Perhaps the second (and fully revised) 1921 edition of Barth's commentary was more revolutionary than the first. But, at any rate, 1919 provides us with a starting point for contemporary theology, and some appreciation of the significance and formative influence of Barth's work on that theology.

That influence is phenomenal. In a sense, it made all twentieth century theology "the theology of crisis." Barth has dominated the theological climate, formulated the theological questions, and been at the center of theological debate since 1919. One Scottish theologian calls him "the greatest figure in modern theology since Schleiermacher."[2] The recently deceased Reinhold Niebuhr has asserted that

1. Quoted in C. Van Til, *The New Modernism* (Philadelphia: Presbyterian and Reformed Publishing Co., 1947), p. 1.
2. T. F. Torrance, "Karl Barth," in *Ten Makers of Modern Protestant Thought*, ed. by George Hunt (New York: Association Press, 1958), p. 58.

Barth is "something of a genius," with "more imagination than any other living theologian."[3] A Methodist professor of theology has endorsed this judgment also. "There is no doubt that Karl Barth has made a stronger impact upon Protestant theology than any other man of the twentieth century, thus far. So varied and far-reaching is his influence that whether one welcomes his ideas or opposes them, one cannot ignore them and still gain even an elementary understanding of the present situation in theology."[4]

What was there in that 1919–1921 commentary that shook the theological world then and now? What new principles had men felt Barth to be emphasizing that became the legacy of a new theological era? Our desire now will be to sketch some of those principles emerging from Barth's commentary that seem to have played the most influential part in the shaping of new theological changes. A more careful analysis of Barth's developed theological perspectives will be outlined in the following chapter.

1. The neo-orthodox revolt against liberalism was one of the most striking features of the early Barth. Barth himself had studied under the great liberal theologians, Harnack and Herrmann, and, until the appearance of his commentary, was part of this world of thought.[5] The Jesus of Barth's teacher, Harnack, was not the unique, supernatural Son of God, but simply the living embodiment of love and humanistic ideals. The Bible of Barth's teacher, Herrmann, was not the infallible Word of God, but an extraordinary yet ordinary book, filled with error, which demanded radical

3. Reinhold Niebuhr, "The Quality of Our Lives," *The Christian Century* LXXVII, 19 (May 11, 1960), 570.

4. L. Harold DeWolf, *Present Trends in Christian Thought* (New York: Association Press, 1960), p. 78 f. An extremely valuable assessment of the significance of Barth's theology from the Reformed standpoint will be found in Fred Klooster's *The Significance of Barth's Theology* (Grand Rapids: Baker Book House, 1961), pp. 11-35.

5. Dale N. Snyder, *Karl Barth's Struggle With Anthropocentric Theology* (The Hague: Boekhandel Wattez, 1966), pp. 25 ff.

criticism to find truth. The yardstick for that truth was experience, feeling. The theology of these men, and of Barth also, was Idealism, marked by a deep streak of pietism and concern for practical Christian experience.

In 1919 and, even more strongly, in the 1921 revision, Barth sought to repudiate much of this classic liberalism. World War I and its horrors helped to shatter his dream world. "Cultured Germany, liberal England, and civilized France were fighting together like mad animals. And hardly had the war begun than Barth's theological teachers joined with others in declaring their support for Germany."[6] Barth's liberal teachers had been unmasked as teachers of a religion sprung from a culture and bound to a culture.

Barth's commentary on Romans sought to repudiate his former teachers. Liberalism called for a God immanent in the world. Barth, in rebellion, pointed to God only as "the Wholly Other."[7] The subjectivism of liberalism in the 19th century had put man in the place of God. Barth shouted, "Let God be God and not man." Liberalism had exalted the cultured use of religion. Barth condemned religion as the supreme sin. Liberalism built theology on the foundation of ethics. Barth wanted to build ethics on the foundation of theology.

2. Barth's 1921 commentary proposed a new view of revelation, one still dominant today. In opposition to the older liberalism, Barth sought to stress man's need for revelation. And, in that spirit, he preferred, above other names for his new ideas, "the Theology of the Word of God." But Barth, in his insistence on revelation, carefully distinguished the Bible from absolute identification with the Word of God. This, as we have already noted, was his Kantian legacy.

---

6. T. H. L. Parker, *Karl Barth* (Grand Rapids: Eerdmans Publishing Co., 1970), p. 16.

7. A full analysis of Barth's early concept of the freedom of God as the Wholly Other will be found in C. Van Til, *op. cit.*, p. 212 ff.

One may read the Bible without hearing the Word of God, says Barth. The Bible is merely a "token," but, at the least, a token through which the Word does come to us. The relationship between God and the Bible remains real, but indirect. "The Bible," says Barth, "is God's Word so far as God speaks through it. . . . The Bible therefore becomes God's Word in this event. . . ."[8] Until it becomes real to us, until it explodes in our life, until it speaks to us in the existential situation, it is not the Word of God. Thus, says Barth, the Bible is a record of past revelation, and a promise of future revelation.

3. Barth's commentary introduced also a new method of explaining theology—dialectic. The name itself quickly became attached to Barth's thinking, though the method itself was borrowed from the writings of the existentialistic philosopher, Kierkegaard.[9] Kierkegaard had said that all theological assertions were paradoxical in character, and could not be synthesized. Man was simply to retain both elements of the paradox in opposition. This act of retention was accomplished in faith (defined as man's highest emotion). The acceptance of the paradox is what has been called "the leap of faith."[10]

Barth was deeply influenced by this concept as he prepared the revisions for his second edition of the Romans commentary.[11] Barth now contended that as long as we are here on earth, we can do no otherwise in theology than proceed by using the method of statement and counter-

---

8. Karl Barth, *Church Dogmatics* (Edinburgh: T. & T. Clark, 1936), I, 1, pp. 123 f.

9. The deeper background to both Kierkegaard and Barth must be the relativistic epistemology of Kant. Francis Schaeffer, on the contrary, appears to place greater formative influence on Hegel (*op. cit.*, pp. 20 ff.).

10. Bernard Ramm, *A Handbook of Contemporary Theology* (Grand Rapids: Eerdmans Publishing Co., 1966), pp. 35-36.

11. Parker, *op. cit.*, pp. 40-43. For a full analysis of Barth's indebtedness to dialectical philosophy, see C. Van Til, *op. cit.*, pp. 43-79.

statement; we dare not pronounce absolutely the final word. . . . Paradox is no accident in Christian theology. It belongs, in some sense, to the heart of doctrinal thinking.

The very nature of revelation, according to Barth, proceeds by means of paradox—God as hidden but revealed; our knowledge of God and our knowledge of sin; every man elect but also reprobate in Christ; Jesus as both the Yes and the No of God; man justified by God and yet, at the same time, a sinner. One commentator has well remarked that, according to the dialectic theology of Barth, revelation coming from above to man, in the contradiction of sin, and within the limits of finitude, can only appear to the human mind as a series of paradoxes.

4. Barth's commentary sought to renew a call for the utter transcendence of God. In fact, Barth's dialectical method seems to be related to his idea that God is always Subject, never Object. God, for Barth, is not one unit in the world of objects: He is the infinite and sovereign "Wholly Other" who is known only as He speaks to us. "He cannot be explained, as an object can; He can only be addressed. . . . For this reason, theology is forbidden to measure Him in direct or unilinear thinking." We cannot speak concerning God. We can only speak to God. According to Barth, the nature of God demands that our statements to Him must always wear the guise of contradiction. "We cannot call Him near except as we call Him far."

Barth's great theme, in alleged opposition to liberalism, was the "infinite qualitative difference" between eternity and time, heaven and earth, God and man. God is not to be identified with anything in the world, not even the words of Scripture. God comes to man, just as the tangent which touches the circle, but does not really touch it. God speaks to man, just as a bombshell which bursts on the earth. After the shell-burst, all that is left is a burnt crater in the ground. Such a crater is the church.

5. Barth's commentary underlined also a new indiffer-ence to history in the world of theology. Nineteenth cen-tury theology had sought to find "the historical Jesus" be-hind the so-called "supernatural Christ" of the Bible. Classic liberals such as Barth's teacher, Harnack, had sought to find kernels of historical facts concerning Jesus in the Gospels, which they condemned as unreliable. Barth denounced this search as a matter of indifference. Revelation does not enter history. It only touches history as a tangent touches a circle. According to Barth (and Bultmann, who still uses these same early ideas), there is nothing in history on which faith could base itself. Faith is a vacuum filled, not from history below, but from revelation above.

Deeply under the influence of Kierkegaard's and Franz Overbeck's views of history, Barth divided history into two levels—*Historie* and *Geschichte* (both words can be trans-lated as simply "history," though their connotations are quite different in German). *Historie* is the sum total of historical facts in the past, which can be objectively verified. *Geschichte* concerns those matters which touch me existen-tially, which make some demand upon me and call for my commitment. According to Barth, the resurrection of Jesus belongs to the realm of *Geschichte*, not *Historie*. In fact, the realm of *Historie* is worthless for the Christian. Jesus must be confronted in the realm of *Geschichte*.[12]

The basic themes of Barth's work on Romans appear again and again in the history of theology that follows in our study. Some seize on one theme and magnify it. Others emphasize another. But their influence remains far-reaching enough to designate the first half of the twentieth century in liberal theology as the world of Barth. Barth himself, in his later work, refined much of this early emphasis and, to

12. For a full analysis of these terms as they are used by Barth, consult Cornelius Van Til, *Christianity and Barthianism* (Phila-delphia: Presbyterian and Reformed Publishing Co., 1962), pp. 13-29.

some extent, smoothed many rough edges.[13] But, like the world of theology that has followed him, he has never escaped its implications, even in his later work.

1. Though Barth's views represent, to some degree, a revolt against classic liberalism, in a deeper sense, Van Til is perfectly accurate in designating his views as "the new modernism." Barth retains the liberal critical view of Scripture. He does not accept the inerrancy of the Bible. In fact, he asserts that the entire Bible is a fallible human document and to seek for infallible parts in Scripture is "mere self-will and disobedience."[14] The inerrancy of Scripture is one of the crucial differences between naturalism and Christianity, and Barth's position places him clearly in the liberal-naturalistic camp.

2. His view of revelation becomes purely subjective in an ultimate sense. The difference between the Bible as merely the Bible and the Bible as the Word of God becomes man's reaction to that book. Moreover, should man, with a leap of faith, hear that voice of God speaking through the "token," man can still not know God as He is. We can know Him only through the paradoxes of dialectic.

3. The end result of Barth's concept of dialectic is to destroy the concept of truth and, with it, the gospel of Christianity. If all non-paradoxical mediation, "all historical communication, all direct experiences of God fit in with a pagan, but not with a Christian conception of God," how can we either approach truth or possess truth in any temporal and

---

13. These refinements can be unduly exaggerated. William Hordern, a sympathetic listener of Barth, admits that "his thought has undergone significant changes. . . ." but he also adds, "there are, however, basic themes that run through his theology so that it has a fundamental consistency," *A Layman's Guide to Protestant Theology* (New York: The Macmillan Co., 1968), p. 132.

14. A fuller critique of Barth's views on Scripture can be found in Colin Brown, *Karl Barth and the Christian Message* (Chicago: Inter-Varsity Press, 1967), pp. 54-62; Klaas Runia, *Karl Barth's Doctrine of Holy Scripture* (Grand Rapids: Eerdmans Publishing Co., 1962).

outward form? How can we, in the same sense, either approach the gospel or possess the gospel in any way? The dialectical method can approximate gospel truth; it cannot convey that truth.

4. In the same way as Barth's dialectical method, his emphasis on God as the Wholly Other makes God, strictly speaking, indescribable. Since God is not an object of time and space, since God is "the Unknown" (to use the language of Kierkegaard), since "Inscrutability . . . hiddenness, belongs to the nature of Him who is called God," man cannot know Him directly. In fact, as Van Til has asked repeatedly, how can man know Him at all?

5. Barth's view of history underlines much of contemporary theology. He finds little of value in the resurrection as an event in what he has called *Historie*, in that realm of reality the newspaper and television refer to as "the daily news." It possesses its most real significance in the realm of *Geschichte*, the realm where man confronts the existential reality of his world in terms of himself, the realm of the person-to-person relationship. Here is a fatal flaw in his view of history. It makes problematic the genuine historicity of the redemptive work of Christ as the foundation for Christianity. In the spirit of Nietzsche and Overbeck, it cuts Christianity from history and, in so doing, destroys the basis for Christianity. To be sure, Barth's purpose in this was to depose the historical method of liberalism from its sovereignty in New Testament study. But in doing so, he also deposed Christianity from its place in history.

The history of contemporary theology repeats one or more of Barth's failures time and time again. Barth could not adequately correct them himself, for his basically Enlightenment, man-centered approach has had no radically biblical emendation.

17

Chapter III

NEO-ORTHODOXY

Karl Barth had unleashed a theological revolution with his work on Romans. In the years that followed, the revolution was refined and enlarged. A movement took shape, often called "neo-orthodoxy," which found expression in the writings of others beside Barth. Emil Brunner (1889–1966) was perhaps the most widely known member of the new school outside of Barth. It even acted as a refining fire and purged away the glossy optimism of liberals like Reinhold Niebuhr (1892–1971).

Barth's own writing did not remain without refinement in the years that followed 1921. But, throughout his shifts and counterattacks, he remained the movement's most well-known spokesman.

Since the early years of Barth's initial work, neo-orthodoxy—or Barthianism—has crossed all national boundaries. Its influence in the Far East, for example, has been very widespread. In Japan, Barth has been described as "a kind of theological pope. . . . Unlike the situation in America, for instance, where Barth has been considered one of the top theologians of this century, in Japan Barth has been regarded as the *only* theologian."[1] This "German capitvity," as Prof. Furuya has called it, first influenced Japan through the writings of Tokutaro Takahura (1885–

---

1. Yasuo Furuya, "The Influence of Barth on Present-day Theological Thought in Japan," *Japan Christian Quarterly* XXX, 4 (October, 1964), p. 262.

1934) about 1924–1925. By 1931, Brunner's *Theology of Crisis* had appeared in Japanese translation, and during the early part of this decade, full-length appraisals of dialectical theology by Japanese theologians were "bestsellers" in the theological world.[2] And through Japan's pre-war colonial program, that neo-orthodox emphasis was planted, or at least encouraged, in the countries in her orbit. Korea showed an awareness of the impact of neo-orthodoxy in the early years of the 1930's, though it was not until liberation in 1945 that it began to form any fully vocal part in the main current of Korean theology.[3] Heresy trials in the late 1940's and early 1950's centered around the neo-orthodox concepts of revelation held by a theological professor, and resulted in disciplinary action against the man. However, by the late 1960's, the newly installed president of the theological seminary of that same denomination could write of modern theology as divided into three main streams—conservative, liberal, and neo-orthodox. And he could add, now with certainty, "I think that the neo-orthodox position follows the thought of the Reformers, catches fully the ear of modern man's sensitivities, and, of the three streams attempting to adhere to orthodox Christian doctrines, is the most reasonable."[4]

One must recognize much diversity in the movement. The sharp difference of opinion between Barth and Brunner over the reality of general revelation and the virgin birth; the criticisms exchanged between Barth and Bultmann; the criticism of Barth's view of history by Pannenberg—all

2. A full appraisal of the rise of dialectical theology in Japan can be found in Charles H. Germany, *Protestant Theologies in Modern Japan* (Tokyo: International Institute for the Study of Religions, 1965), pp. 87-155.

3. Kan Ha-bae, "Korean Theology—Where Is It Going?," *Themelios* VII, 1 (Spring, 1970), 33-36; Harvie M. Conn, "Studies in the Theology of the Korean Presbyterian Church—Part III," *Westminster Theological Journal* XXX, 1 (November, 1967), 45-59.

4. Rhee Jong-sung, *The Layman and Theology* (Seoul: Presbyterian General Assembly Education Committee, 1969), pp. 14-15.

these things indicate that there is not always one voice in the movement. Yet, at the same time, there is too much of an underlying superstructure to say simply that Barth denies general revelation while Brunner accepts it, or that Brunner denies the virgin birth while Barth accepts it.[5] In an earlier chapter, we have indicated some of the presuppositions and methodology of modern theological structure. Our emphasis now must be on the common themes. And regrettably we must continue merely to sketch. The model for our sketch will be Barth's series on *Church Dogmatics*, now reaching over 8,000 pages (begun in 1932 and unfinished at Barth's death).

1. As we saw in the previous chapter, one of the main themes of neo-orthodoxy remains the concept of revelation. Revelation, according to Barth, is "a perpendicular from above" and cannot be equated with the best insights of man. It is an event in which God takes the initiative. At the same time, revelation, it is said, is not to be equated with the Bible. The Bible and its statements are witnesses, signs, pointers of revelation. The Word of God is not the Scripture itself, nor are the statements of Scripture themselves the revelation. According to Barth, to equate the Bible with the Word of God is "an objectifying and materializing of revelation."

In this same connection, Brunner especially has emphasized revelation as event. It is an event which calls for both the Speaker and the hearer. Revelation "is not understood as the delivery of truths about God but as an event or an occasion or a dialogue in which God encounters man. Revelation cannot be said to have taken place unless both partners of the encounter enter into the encounter."[6]

5. This absence of deeper reflection on the foundational framework seems manifest, we tend to feel, in the judgments of Klaas Runia on some of these areas in his book, *Reformation Today* (London: Banner of Truth Trust, 1968), pp. 14 ff.

6. For a fuller analysis, compare Paul Schrotenboer, "Emil Brunner," *Creative Minds in Contemporary Theology*, ed. by Philip

2. The heart of revelation, of the Word of God, is Jesus Christ. In fact, Barth is so insistent on this that he refuses to recognize the existence of any revelation apart from his Christ. The history of revelation and the history of salvation become the same history.

In Barth's Christ, God revealed that He was not willing to let man exist in sin. Thus Barth insists that we should never mention sin unless we immediately go on to say that sin has been overcome, forgiven, and defeated in Jesus, the elect one. The reconciliation between God and man is effected by the event of Jesus Christ. Jesus Christ is very God, that is, the God who humbles himself. In His freedom, God crosses the yawning abyss and shows He is truly the Lord. God "sets at stake His own existence as God."[7] Barth is not willing to admit the humiliation of the man, Jesus. According to Barth, to say that humiliation concerns man is mere tautology. "What sense could there be in speaking of man as humiliated? This is natural to man. But to say that God humiliates Himself, according to Barth, is to understand the real meaning of Jesus Christ as very God."[8]

3. Barth refuses to admit the traditional view of the two states of Christ—the humiliation of Christ and the exaltation of Christ—as following one another chronologically. Jesus as very God humbled himself, and Jesus as very man was exalted. To Barth, to say that exaltation as a state concerns God is also mere tautology. What sense can there be in speaking of God as exalted? This is natural to God. According to Barth, "In Christ humanity is exalted humanity, just as Godhead is humiliated Godhead. And humanity is exalted by the humiliation of Godhead."[9]

Hughes (Grand Rapids: Eerdmans Publishing Co., 1966), pp. 104-107.

7. Karl Barth, *Church Dogmatics* (Edinburgh: T. & T. Clark, 1956), IV, 1, p. 72.

8. Klooster, *op. cit.*, p. 88.

9. Karl Barth, *Church Dogmatics* (Edinburgh: T. & T. Clark, 1957), II, 2, p. 103.

4. One of the most controversial features of neo-orthodoxy has been its ambiguity regarding the possibility of universal salvation. Barth has said that "in its simplest and most comprehensive form the dogma of predestination consists . . . in the assertion that the divine predestination is the election of Jesus Christ."[10] Jesus is not only the Elector, He is also the Elected. Jesus in fact is also the only Elected. And in Christ, *all* men are elect and *all* men are reprobate. Barth rejects the classic concept of double predestination, the idea of an election with reference to individuals. He admits that all men do not live as elect men, and still others may do so only partially. However, the responsibility of the church is to proclaim to such men that they have been all elected in Christ, and now therefore must live as elect. No opposition to the gospel is absolute for Barth. Election is not a status we obtain in Christ. Election is action, service for God. There are no frontiers to cross from rejection to election. There is only non-recognition of election, and recognition of election.

Does this imply universal salvation in neo-orthodoxy? Barth himself does not seem either to affirm or to deny the theory. His most recent lectures on *The Humanity of God* ended a discussion of this question by saying, "We have no theological right to set any limits to the loving kindness of God which has appeared in Jesus Christ. Our theological duty is to see and understand it as being still greater than we had seen before."[11]

For many reasons, neo-orthodoxy has been misunderstood by many Christians. It claims to be a return to the teaching of the Reformers. It claims to attack the optimism of classic liberalism and the corruptions of Roman Catholic theology. It claims to emphasize strongly the absolute centrality of Jesus Christ, the transcendence of God, the neces-

10. *Loc. cit.*
11. Karl Barth, *The Humanity of God* (Richmond: John Knox Press, 1960), pp. 61-62.

22

sity of revelation. Naturally, all of these emphases would sound very congenial to the evangelical Christian.

But, as many have pointed out, neo-orthodoxy departs from the historic Christian faith not merely in many areas but in its root conceptions. In no way can it be called "a return to the teachings of the Reformation." Some of its more glaring faults include the following items.

1. Neo-orthodoxy's center turns upon the subjective experience of man as a criterion of truth. So, in neo-orthodoxy, revelation is not simply the declaration of God to man. Revelation is said to be meeting, confrontation, dialogue. The Bible is not revelation until it becomes revelation to us. This is to destroy the very concept of revelation itself. It is especially here that one sees the indebtedness of neo-orthodoxy to the so-called existentialist school of philosophy.

2. In keeping with this same refusal to identify the Bible with revelation or the Word of God, neo-orthodoxy retains the language of orthodox theology but reinterprets it. And this reinterpretation produces much the same results as poison in the milk. Original sin, Adam and the fall, redemption in Christ, the resurrection, the second coming, are called myth by Brunner and saga by Barth. It is said that these historical events have no impact on the basis of their having once happened. They are not so much facts as existential conditions under which all men exist. Using the language of Barth's philosophy of history which we introduced in chapter two, they are not *Historie* but *Geschichte*. Genesis 3, for example, is not to be taken as literal history. It is, say Barth and Niebuhr, only pointing, in a symbolic way, to the reality of sin and pride in the human life. This concept of neo-orthodoxy destroys the central meaning of the gospel as "good news," as the proclamation of the coming of God's Son into this world of history for the salvation of sinners.

3. Barth's insistence on Jesus Christ as the heart of

23

revelation is so strong that he denies the existence of any revelation of God apart from Christ in nature. This view does serious damage to more than the reality of general revelation (Acts 14:17; Rom. 1:19-20). It is not merely stress or emphasis on special revelation at the expense of natural revelation. It involves a complete reinterpretation of every form of revelation, and with it a destruction of the biblical character of revelation itself.

4. Barth's refusal to speak of the humiliation of Jesus as very man leaves him open to the charge of theopaschitism, and involves a radical departure from biblical theology.[12] He is unwilling to distinguish carefully between the person and work of Christ in any ontological sense, and by thus repudiating the Chalcedon Creed, Barth's handling of the work of Christ destroys the person of Christ in an activistic way.[13] In fact, in Barth's view, "the incarnation is the really crucial thing in reconciliation by which the gulf between God and man is bridged. . . . The biblical emphasis upon our being reconciled to God through the death of His Son (Rom. 5:10; Col. 1:22) and his having made peace through the blood of the cross (Col. 1:20; Eph. 2:16) does not really fit into Barth's doctrine of reconciliation."[14]

5. Though Barth claims neither to affirm nor to deny the theory of universal salvation, it seems that his idea of universal election clearly implies some sort of "neo-universalism." In fact, his rejection of the realities of heaven and hell would also point to a concept of salvation radically different from the one set forth in the Scriptures. Jesus, says Barth, is the history of salvation for every man, the circle of salvation Daniel Niles finds large enough to include Buddhists, Confucianists, Shintoists. The frontier

12. G. C. Berkouwer, *The Triumph of Grace in the Theology of Karl Barth* (Grand Rapids: Eerdmans Publishing Co., 1956), pp. 125-135, 297-327.

13. Cornelius Van Til, *Karl Barth on Chalcedon* (Philadelphia: Presbyterian and Reformed Publishing Co., 1960).

14. Klooster, *op. cit.*, p. 96.

from election to rejection, and vice versa, can be repeatedly crossed and crisscrossed.

The result of such a position destroys the seriousness of unbelief. And, in this way, neo-orthodoxy destroys the scriptural warnings against apostasy as well as the call to repentance and faith. The total impact of the Barthian theology "tones down the desperateness of the sinner's situation as described in the Scriptures. . . . His view simply calls for informing men who are universally involved in what Christ has done. Hence the urgency of preaching is gone, and the biblical significance of the call to repentance and faith loses its relevance."[15]

---

15. *Ibid.*, pp. 70-71.

CHAPTER IV

FORM CRITICISM—BULTMANN'S METHOD

The same year Karl Barth published his commentary on Romans, two other books appeared on New Testament themes, heralding a new shift in critical studies. From one of the books, *Die Formgeschichte des Evangeliums*, penned by Martin Dibelius (1883–1947), came the name of the movement, Form Criticism. From the other title by Karl L. Schmidt, *Der Rahmen der Geschichte Jesu* (1919) came the final blow from liberal circles to the reliability of what had been commonly accepted till now concerning the historical framework of Mark's Gospel.

But even more than these two men, the heart of this new shift in studies came to be associated largely with one man. The man was Rudolf Bultmann (1884–) and the book which transformed New Testament studies was *History of the Synoptic Tradition* (1921). Even more than Dibelius, Bultmann's influence has continued to expand. In particular, it has been Bultmann's method as well as (sometimes more than) his message that has found wide usage. So, many like Oscar Cullmann and Joachim Jeremias, though critical of the results of Bultmann's own studies, can reach their own conclusions by an adaptation of the methods Bultmann has helped to pioneer. And especially in England and the United States, scholars, though "wary of the discipline which was associated almost exclusively with the name of Bultmann," and stressing the limitations of form criticism as such, still have come "slowly and cautiously to an acceptance of the basic presupposition of the form critics."[1]

This acceptance has not been limited to the Western world. Japan is giving Bultmann's method a new hearing. One younger professor of theology there recently commented that "it is one of Bultmann's contributions that he has criticized the contents of the New Testament. We are no longer likely to accept what the New Testament says just because it says so. We are critically to reflect on whether what the New Testament says is true or false historically."[2] In Korea, particularly during the last ten years, the influence of Bultmann's techniques has grown.[3] The methodology of form criticism has been warmly received and used to varying degrees by such New Testament scholars as Dr. Chun Kyung-yun of the Hankuk Theological Seminary and, more recently, Prof. Pak Chang-hwan of the Presbyterian Theological Seminary, Seoul.

1. The presupposition of form criticism is that the Bible cannot be relied upon as a trustworthy account of the life and teachings of Christ and His apostles. In the language of a contemporary form critic, "the work of the Form Critic was designed to show that the message of Jesus as given to us in the Synoptics is, for the most part, not authentic, but was minted by the faith of the primitive Christian community in its various stages." For Bultmann, the Bible is not the inspired Word of God in any objective sense. While God speaks to men through the Bible, "objectively the Bible is a product of the ancient historical and religious influences and must be evaluated exactly like any other ancient religious literature."[4]

---

1. E. V. McKnight, *What Is Form Criticism* (Philadelphia: Fortress Press, 1969), p. 56.

2. Yoshio Noro, "Transcendence and Immanence in Contemporary Theology: A Report Article," *Northeast Asia Journal of Theology* (Sept., 1969), p. 64.

3. Kan Ha-bae, *op. cit.*, p. 36.

4. This presupposition is carefully analyzed by Herman Ridderbos,

2. The fundamental assumption of form criticism is that the Gospels are primarily products of the editing work of the early Christian church. The gospel writers sought to link together various contradictory, independent oral traditions circulating in the church before the time of the writing of the New Testament. These oral traditions are not even themselves totally reliable. They consisted basically of individual sayings and narratives concerning Jesus and His disciples. The church used them and tied them together in narrative form, inventing locations, times, and linkings to bind the independent traditions together. Such phrases in the Gospels as "on a ship," "immediately," "the next day," "on a journey"—are all said to be simply literary devices used by the gospel editors to unite all the independent sayings and stories about Jesus. As K. L. Schmidt, one of the pioneers in this method, has said, "We do not have the story of Jesus, we only have stories about Jesus."[5]

3. The purpose of the form critical method is to analyze the history of the oral tradition underlying the written Gospels. The Gospels serve us only as the raw material for our study to find "the gospel before the gospels."[6] Since the assumption is that the early church has organized artificially, according to its own apologetic and evangelistic purposes, the material of the Gospels into one harmonious account, the form critic must destroy that artificial harmony, try to discover the original forms of the oral tradition now embedded in the writing, and then reconstruct the earliest tradition as best he can.[7]

4. The first step in this technique is to admit that any

Bultmann (Philadelphia: Presbyterian and Reformed Publishing Co., 1960), pp. 10-14.

5. K. L. Schmidt, *Der Rahmen der Geschichte Jesu* (Berlin: Trowitzsch, 1919), p. 317.

6. The title of one of the earlier works by American form critic, B. S. Easton, dealing with the technique (New York: Scribners, 1928).

7. McKnight, *op. cit.*, pp. 17 ff.

indications in the Gospels of sequence, time, place, etc., are unhistorical and untrustworthy. We must pare away the framework of the story to find the bare skeleton of the beginning, the detached anecdotes and teachings artificially strung together by the early church.

5. When this has been done, the individual passages are classified into such groups as miracle stories, controversial sayings, prophecies, apophthegmata. Each of these groups has a certain fixed form. Thus, if one finds the individual tradition more or less similar to this fixed form, one can judge whether it belongs to a primary or secondary tradition, to an earlier or later source, to a more or less reliable tradition. As one writer has described it, "the form critic determines the age of gospel stories and sayings by looking at their forms in the same way as a horse dealer tells the age of horses by looking at their teeth."[8] The older an account is, the more reliable it is as a historical source.

6. The results of this sort of methodology are highly inducive of skepticism, to say the least. For Bultmann, the historical residuum is found largely in the teachings of Jesus, not in the record of His deeds, and even less so in the portrayal of His person. He does not doubt that Jesus lived and did many of the works attributed to Him in the analyzed tradition. But he is skeptical about everything else. He writes, "I do indeed think that we can now know almost nothing concerning the life and personality of Jesus, since the early Christian sources show no interest in either, are moreover fragmentary and legendary; and other sources about Jesus do not exist."[9]

For the orthodox Christian, there are formal points of contact between himself and some of Bultmann's emphases. (1) Form criticism reminds us that the gospel was, in fact,

---

8. Compare Kan Ha-bae, "The New Quest for the Historical Jesus," *Themelios* VI, 2 (1969), 25-40.
9. Rudolf Bultmann, *Jesus and the Word* (New York: Scribners, 1958), p. 8.

29

preserved for a generation in oral form before it was reduced to writing in the New Testament. (2) Form criticism also reminds us that the Gospels are not "neutral, impartial" records, but witnesses to the faith of Christian believers. (3) Form criticism has failed to discover a non-supernatural Jesus. All of the New Testament documents, no matter how form criticism cuts them up, still reflect a supernatural Jesus, the Son of God. (4) Form criticism reminds us of the occasional character of the Gospels. They were written with a view to the particular historical occasion and situation— Matthew to the Jews, Mark and Luke to the Gentiles. As such, they do express a concern for the life situation in which they were written, and in which they were concerned. (5) Form criticism reminds us that the Gospels are not nearly as much interested in geographical details and chronological details as even the orthodox community had formerly thought.

But all these points of contact with orthodox Christian views of the gospel are ultimately superficial. Like Barth, Bultmann's method itself does radical injustice to the nature of the New Testament in basic ways.

1. Although it is true that the Gospels do not always give a chronicle of continuous events, it does not mean, as form criticism argues, that there is no trustworthy historical outline for the life of Christ. Within the limits of a broad historical outline, each evangelist arranged his material to serve his own purpose. It is poor criticism to demand from the gospel writers what they do not intend. And it is poor criticism to insist that what they did intend is not historical or trustworthy. Luke's prologue (Luke 1:1-4) is a clear indication of the gospel writers' concern to root their narrative in history. The Gospels remain good news.[10]

---

10. B. Van Elderen, "The Teaching of Jesus and the Gospel Records," in *Jesus of Nazareth: Saviour and Lord*, ed. by C. F. H. Henry (Grand Rapids: Eerdmans Publishing Co., 1966), pp. 111-119.

2. Form criticism does injustice to the writers of the gospel records. Matthew, Mark, and Luke are reduced to mere editors of documents, and the Gospels to self-contradictory records. All this does radical injustice to the unity of the gospel record. The Gospels possess a basic unity as trustworthy witnesses to Christ. Actually, the several Gospels do not present diverse frameworks for the life of Jesus. Rather, each Gospel is a witness to certain aspects of the single historical framework of Christ's life which has not been completely preserved. Form criticism does not recognize the diversity of oral transmission within the unity of the gospel records.[11]

3. Form criticism separates Christianity from Christ. The great assumption of this method of study is that the Christian community, not Christ, exercised the major creative role in the production of the Gospels. However, the message of the New Testament is centered, not in the community, but in Christ. (II Cor. 4:5). The church, like Paul and his fellow apostles, was witness, not creator (I Cor. 4:1-2). Its major responsibility was not creation of new traditions, but the preservation and proclamation of the old ones.

4. Form criticism separates Christianity from the apostles. Bultmann and others completely discount the presence of the apostles as the guardians of the accurate tradition in the early church concerning Jesus. The apostles were an authoritative source of information about the facts and doctrines of Christianity and of Christ. Acts 1:21-22 underlines this strategic control the apostles exercised over the spread of the gospel in these years of oral transmission. Their presence was intended to prevent the occurrence of precisely the situation described by form criticism. The apostles were God's guarantee of the continuity and integrity of the historic Christian faith.

11. Ned B. Stonehouse, *Paul Before the Areopagus* (Grand Rapids: Eerdmans Publishing Co., 1957), pp. 123 ff.

5. Form criticism seems oblivious to the small time lag separating the historical facts and the written documents. Mark's Gospel was written in the 60's, if not the 50's. Paul received his account of the tradition in the mid-30's (Gal. 1:18). Many of the apostles and eye-witnesses of Jesus lived throughout the entire period in which the Gospels were written. Where is the time for the collection, creation, and circulation of these community "sagas" and "myths"? The events of Jesus' life were not hidden from public view (Acts 26:26). There were witnesses for both the defense and the attack on Christianity. The gospel exploded into life in the midst of well-attested history. Form criticism cannot explain this at all.

CHAPTER V

DEMYTHOLOGIZATION: BULTMANN'S MESSAGE

One of the key words for understanding twentieth century theology is "demythologization." The term was made famous by Rudolf Bultmann, when he introduced the idea in a 1941 essay.[1]

The impact of the concept in Europe has been tremendous. And though, in some respects, Germany does not seem to be as interested in the concept as before, in the United States and Asia interest is growing. The idea was given new encouragement when Bishop John Robinson of England popularized it in his 1963 book, *Honest to God.*

Not all of Bultmann's thought may, by any means, be summed up in this phrase. In the previous chapter, we have tried to indicate another very significant part of Bultmann's influence today. However, the demythologization program is certainly a significant part of the professor's theology and the part which today remains most debated.

1. The center of the program is Bultmann's contention that one finds two things in the New Testament—(1) the Christian gospel, and (2) the first century world view, mythological in character. The gospel essence, what Bultmann calls the kerygma (a transliteration of the Greek word meaning "the content of what is preached"), is the irreducible core with which our modern age must be confronted and which we must believe. However, modern man cannot

---

1. Rudolf Bultmann, "New Testament and Mythology," *Kerygma and Myth* (London: SPCK, 1953).

accept the mythical framework in which the gospel essence is wrapped. So "theology must undertake the task of stripping the kerygma from its mythical framework."[2] According to Bultmann, this "mythical framework" is not specifically Christian, anyway.

2. "Myth" for Bultmann is the undifferentiated discourse of a pre-scientific age.[3] It is the purpose of myth to express man's understanding of himself, not to present an objective picture of the world. Myth uses imagery and terms taken from this world to express these convictions of man's self-understanding. So, in the first century, the Jew understood his world as a system open to God and supernatural powers. The universe in the first century was said to be three-storied, with heaven above, the earth, and hell below the earth. Bultmann contends that this is the world-view contained in the Bible. The order of nature is one frequently disturbed by supernatural intervention.

3. This mythical transformation of the world also has been used to transform Jesus, according to Bultmann. The historical person of Jesus was very soon turned into a myth in primitive Christianity, and so "Bultmann argues that an historical knowledge of the man Jesus is irrelevant to Christian faith."[4] It is this myth which confronts us in the New Testament picture of Jesus. The historical facts about Jesus are said to have been transformed into the mythical story of a divine preexistent being who became incarnate and atoned by his blood for the sins of men, rose from the dead, ascended into heaven, and would, as was believed, shortly return to judge the world and inaugurate the new age. This central story is also embellished allegedly by miracle stories, stories about voices from heaven, victories

2. *Ibid.*, p. 3.
3. There is an excellent discussion and critique of Bultmann's myth concept in Philip E. Hughes, *Scripture and Myth* (London: The Tyndale Press, 1956).
4. Hordern, *op. cit.*, p. 201.

over demons, etc. We must remember that Bultmann claims all of this presentation of Jesus in the New Testament is not history but myth, that is, the thought patterns of people who created these myths to understand themselves better. They are myths which have no validity for twentieth century man, who believes in hospitals and not miracles, penicillin and not prayers. To communicate the gospel effectively to modern man, we must strip off the myth from the New Testament and try to uncover the original purpose behind the myth. That process of uncovering is "demythologization."

4. This process does not mean denying the mythology, according to Bultmann. It means interpreting it existentially, that is, in terms of man's understanding of his own existence, and in those terms modern man himself can understand. Bultmann does this by using the concepts of the German existentialist philosopher, Martin Heidegger (1889–).[5] So, for example, the alleged myth of the virgin birth of Christ is said to be an attempt to express the meaning of Jesus for faith. "They say that Christ comes to us as the action of God."[6] The cross of Christ has no significance with regard to the vicarious bearing of sins by Jesus for others. It has significance only as a symbol of man's taking up a new existence, giving up all our worldly security for a new life that is lived out of the transcendent.[7]

5. Ultimately, Bultmann says that the basic features of New Testament mythology center on two kinds of self-understanding. One is life outside of faith and one is life in faith. The terms sin, flesh, fear, and death are mythological explanations of this life outside of faith. In existential

5. The fullest discussion of the relationships between Heidegger and Bultmann can be found in: John Macquarrie, *An Existentialist Theology* (London: SCM Press, 1955). For a Reformed critique of this indebtedness, consult Robert D. Knudsen, "Bultmann," in *Creative Minds in Contemporary Theology, op. cit.*, pp. 131 ff.

6. Hordern, *op. cit.*, p. 205.

7. Ridderbos, *op. cit.*, pp. 23-26.

terms, it is said to mean life in bondage to tangible, visible realities which perish.

Life in faith, on the other hand, means abandoning this adherence to visible, tangible realities. It means release from one's own past and openness to God's future. According to Bultmann, this is eschatology's only real meaning. True eschatological living is said to be living in constant renewal through decision and obedience.

Bultmann helps to remind us of the necessity of understanding modern man as we preach to him. And he reminds us also of the necessity of making sure that we carefully apply the gospel as well as simply proclaim it. In this connection, it is interesting that such Korean scholars as Prof. Ryu Tong-shik and Dr. Yun Sung-bum make much use of Bultmann's approach to hermeneutics in their discussion of so-called "indigenization of theology."[8] They have recognized that Bultmann is grappling with very similar problems.

But, for several reasons, our judgment of demythologization must be negative.

1. "Demythologization" is, like neo-orthodoxy, strongly indebted to a school of philosophy, existentialism, radically at odds with the New Testament itself. One is deeply man-centered in its approach, the other deeply God-centered. By adapting such man-centered categories in his efforts to have the New Testament tell us something about human existence, Bultmann not only does great injustice to the God-centered character of Christianity. He also loses the only center by which man in his essence can be understood properly. The real purpose of the New Testament is to proclaim that the sovereign God has come, and He has come in Christ to restore man's proper nature as image of God. The heart of the New Testament remains not man but God.

2. "Demythologization" destroys the foundation of Chris-

---

8. Kan Ha-bae, *op. cit.*, pp. 41-42.

tianity in history. The religion of the Bible becomes a religion founded on myths. Herman Ridderbos remarks that, according to Bultmann, Jesus "was not conceived by the Holy Ghost, not born of the virgin Mary. He did suffer under Pontius Pilate, he was crucified. He did not descend into hell. He did not rise again on the third day from the dead; He did not ascend into heaven. He does not sit on the right hand of God the Father and He will not come again to judge the living and the dead."[9] According to Bultmann, these words are devoid of any literal meaning. They are mythological, and do not denote any historical, objective reality. This is also true of the Trinity, the substitutionary atonement, justification, and the work of the Holy Spirit.

3. Primitive Christianity is stamped by the impact of the person and work of Christ. No other explanation can possibly account for the rise of the church and its theology. But Bultmann reduces Jesus' influence to nothing. He assumes that virtually all reliable recollection about Jesus was either annihilated or suppressed in the brief period that separated His earthly life from the period of gospel preaching. Such skepticism is untenable. It must be remembered that Jesus the Teacher was greater than the disciple-community which he taught.

4. "Demythologization," like classic liberalism, leads to a radical skepticism regarding New Testament supernaturalism. And, for this very reason, it is often called "neo-liberalism."[10] Bultmann's program demands nothing less than a radical rejection of the supernaturalism of classic Christianity. Every doctrine that Bultmann calls myth, the New Testament calls fact. All this is quite in keeping with Bultmann's anthropocentric emphasis. But it is radically

---

9. Ridderbos, *op. cit.*, pp. 26-46.
10. This designation is often a part of Reformed vocabulary (cf. K. Runia, *loc. cit.*, for examples of such usage). The danger is that it may tend to differentiate too sharply the presuppositions of Bultmann from Barth.

opposed to the theocentric character of the New Testament.

5. Bultmann's assumption that the relevance of the gospel will become apparent to modern man ignores the depravity of the human heart. It is not "demythologization," but the Holy Spirit who can dispel the darkness of unbelief and cause the sinner to see the gospel. No matter what efforts are made to apply the gospel (whether good or bad), to the "natural man, the things of the Spirit will remain foolishness" (I Cor. 2:14).

CHAPTER VI

HEILSGESCHICHTE

Part of the twentieth century world of theology revolves around a German word, *Heilsgeschichte*, usually translated as something like "salvation history." The man who has given that word its fullest meaning for contemporary Western theology is a Swiss New Testament scholar, Dr. Oscar Cullmann (1902–). Though its meaning and roots go back to such nineteenth century German scholars as J. C. K. von Hofmann and Adolf Schlatter, Dr. Cullmann is the man who has become its most widely known spokesman in our contemporary world. In fact, one British theologian speaks of one of Cullmann's books as "one of the six most important books in recent decades."[1]

Placing our study of Cullmann and *Heilsgeschichte* at this point in our book has some significance. For at least two principal theologians we have already introduced have deeply affected Cullmann's arguments by way of reaction and inter-reaction. From Karl Barth, Cullmann's *Heilsgeschichte* concept has borrowed many basic ideas for a new approach to history. From Barth also has come an emphasis on the indispensability of a Christocentric understanding of the New Testament and the concept of the definitive role of faith in divine revelation. From Rudolf Bultmann, Cullmann has borrowed the exegetical methods of form criticism in his reconstruction of the history of New

1. A. M. Hunter, *Interpreting the New Testament 1900–1950* (Philadelphia: The Westminster Press, 1951), pp. 126 ff.

Testament Christianity. Because of this relationship, there is much wisdom in referring to Cullmann's insights as neo-orthodox in direction.

At the same time, Cullmann has not been afraid to dis-associate himself from these men. He himself claims that Barth and Bultmann have swallowed alien philosophical notions "to corrupt their grasp of the spontaneous and inde-pendent message of the New Testament."[2] According to Cullmann, the impulse of Bultmann particularly in dis-tinguishing between the accidental and the essential elements of the message of the New Testament is arbitrary and naive. The New Testament, he says, must be understood on its own terms.

This difference between Cullmann and his theological influences may help to explain why many of his ideas have been much more acceptable among Western evangelicals than those of his fellow Barthians. His writings seek to be less dependent on existentialism and other philosophi-cal presuppositions, more dependent on scriptural exegesis, than the work of Barth or Bultmann. He seems to have tried harder than any of these men to subject his interpreta-tions to the test of Scripture. He has been a strong opponent of many of the radical features of form criticism and de-mythologization. And, in this same connection, he has repeatedly stressed the importance of history for a proper understanding of the Bible. Though his concept of history is radically at odds with the evangelical, his formal emphasis on the central idea of "salvation history," that God acts in history, is an emphasis most congenial to orthodox the-ology. And still another emphasis of this approach formally similar to biblical theology is its strong emphasis on Chris-tology. One of Cullmann's most useful books is an exegeti-cal study of the titles of Christ in the New Testament. In it,

---

2. David H. Wallace, "Oscar Cullmann," in *Creative Minds in Contemporary Theology, op. cit.*, p. 168.

he claims, that "early Christian theology is in reality almost exclusively Christology."[3]

Several of the major features of the *Heilsgeschichte* school may be outlined as follows:

1. The great emphasis of *Heilsgeschichte* is on history and the revelation of God in history. Time is the arena where God acts to accomplish man's salvation in Christ. Divine revelation and redemption are based on historical realities, not church-invented myths, as Bultmann contends.

2. However, this underlining of history as a vehicle for revelation is said to mean that Scripture is not the ultimate datum of the Christian religion. The ultimate datum is holy history. Scripture is understood as merely the record of that more ultimate datum, not the reality itself. As George Ernest Wright, an Old Testament scholar belonging to this same school, has said, revelation is given in historical deeds, not words.[4] The New Testament is to be understood as a testimony to God's acts of deed-revelation.

3. The central deed in this salvation-history is the first coming of Jesus Christ as Saviour. All history and all time, according to Cullmann, are a world drama, and Jesus Christ is the central figure in that drama. The Jews in the time of the New Testament looked to the coming of the Messiah-Saviour as the announcement of the imminent end of the world, the center of history, after which the glories of "the age to come" would be introduced. The Bible affirmed that the Messiah was Jesus of Nazareth and that in Him the new age did, in fact, begin.

4. This means a new perspective on eschatology. For Cullmann, eschatology embraces all saving events beginning

---

3. Oscar Cullmann, *The Christology of the New Testament* (Philadelphia: The Westminster Press, 1959), pp. 2-3.

4. George Ernest Wright, *God Who Acts* (London: SCM Press, 1952), pp. 11 ff. For a careful critique of *Heilsgeschichte* studies in the Old Testament, consult Edward Young, *The Study of Old Testament Theology Today* (London: James Clarke and Co., 1958), pp. 15 ff.

with the incarnation and concluding with the second coming. The blessings of the age to come have been introduced already by the work and witness of Christ, but their completion and consummation await the time of the second coming when the kingdom of God will be fully present in all its power and glory. The church has entered the final phase of the divine plan of redemption. The battle that decides the final victory has already taken place. In this way, all history is seen as a cosmic drama, with the narrow line of biblical history as the key to the action. The offense of the gospel, according to Cullmann, is its claim that we should take this slender line of sacred history as the clue to all history.

5. An interpreter is said to know this history only as he identifies himself with it. It is especially here that the salvation-history school shows its neo-orthodox presuppositions. History remains history and not revelation, if the student does not participate in this history by faith. In spite of a strong emphasis on biblical history, these men still "hesitate to regard the meaning of salvation as objectively given and accessible. Instead, they continue to speak of religious experience or decision as a fulcrum of revelation."[5]

As we have indicated already, in many areas, the emphasis of Cullmann and the *Heilsgeschichte* school formally resembles orthodox theology. His strong emphasis on salvation as a historical event centered in Christ is a useful reminder in view of form criticism's program of demythologization. His insights into the relation between the first coming of Christ and eschatology have been especially useful in correcting even certain orthodox emphases in the past. His own exegetical insights into the Scriptures are also a significant part of his contribution to biblical studies.

At the same time, the evangelical must be aware of the fact that Cullmann's basic working presuppositions are those

---

5. Carl F. H. Henry, *Frontiers in Modern Theology* (Chicago: Moody Press, 1966), pp. 44-45.

of Barth and Bultmann and therefore display some striking disabilities in connection with his approach to salvation history. His very concern to remain close to the original text comes because of his basic conviction that history is always impregnated with myth.

1. Although Cullmann is critical of the skeptical results of Bultmann's form criticism, and although he himself feels these methods "help us draw nearer to the historical Jesus," he also concedes that the technique of form criticism "establishes the deviation of the early Christian community from Jesus as its object."[6] In short, form criticism discloses the Bible as a product of the early Christian community and not a totally reliable account of the life and teaching of Jesus. Regardless of Cullmann's own criticism of Bultmann's use of form criticism, ultimately his use also often makes a separation between the Bible and the Word of God. So, for example, he calls the biblical accounts of creation and the second coming "myths." He is not completely willing to admit the reality of revelation as inscripturated, infallible truth.

2. In connection with Cullmann's views on revelation, we should also note that he is still strongly dependent on the subjectivism of neo-orthodoxy.[7] Classic Reformed theology has insisted that the illuminating work of the Holy Spirit is necessary for man to understand God's revelation (I Cor. 2:14). The *Heilsgeschichte* scholar believes that, unless man understands, it is not even revelation. As Carl F. H. Henry has said, "they suspend the knowability of the meaning of revelation upon subjective decision and isolate it from divine truths and doctrines objectively and authoritatively given in the inspired Scriptures."[8]

---

6. Oscar Cullmann, "An Autobiographical Sketch," *Scottish Journal of Theology* XIV, 3 (Sept., 1961), p. 233.

7. Van Til, *The Great Debate Today, op. cit.*, pp. 33-42, offers an excellent analysis of Cullmann's framework of thought.

8. Henry, *op. cit.*, p. 46.

3. To concentrate exclusively on God's acts as media of revelation ignores several important facts. (a) Deeds are mute for us unless they are accompanied by word-revelation concerning their significance. *Heilsgeschichte* does not give verbal communication its proper place. (b) The neglect of word revelation overlooks the place which the communication of truth occupies in the history of salvation. As Professor John Murray has indicated, salvation is the salvation of the whole man. And this includes the enlightenment of the mind. "But how can redemption be effective in the whole range of personal life without the correction which truth conveyed imparts, without the enlightenment which truth sheds abroad in mind and heart?"[9] The Bible is true to this need. *Heilsgeschichte* is not.

4. Cullmann builds a philosophy of time and history in Christ. But he so strongly concentrates on the work of Christ that he denies, by neglect, the ontological deity of Christ, thus denying the Christ of Scriptures. He repeatedly insists that the New Testament has almost no interest in the ontological person of Christ. Ultimately, then, the Christ of Cullmann is no more the Christ of Scriptures than the Christ of Barth.

For this reason, he faces the danger of making Christianity so almost exclusively christological that it becomes Christomonism (a common fault with Karl Barth), thus rejecting through neglect the historic Christian formulations of the doctrine of the Trinity. It is true that the theology of the early church was richly colored by Christology (II Cor. 13:13). But it was basically a trinitarian theology (Rom. 8:31-39; John 1:18; I Cor. 15:28).

5. Cullmann contends that eternity is simply unending time. By arguing this way, he seems to destroy any real significant distinction between time and eternity. Eternity,

---

9. John Murray, "Systematic Theology—II," *Westminster Theological Journal* XXVI, 1 (Nov., 1963), 36-38.

or "eternal life," is not simply life of unending time, as Cullmann insists. It is the life of the age to come, which will follow this age (Dan. 12:2). When the rich young ruler asked how to inherit eternal life (Mark 10:17), he was thinking of the life of the resurrection, and Jesus answered him in the same terms. This eternal life is the life of the kingdom of God (10:23), which will be inherited in the age to come (Mark 10:30; Matt. 25:46). So also in Paul, eternal life is the final eschatological goal of the entire redemptive process (Rom. 6:22; Titus 3:7). One finds the same emphasis in John's Gospel (3:36; 5:39; 17:25).

6. Cullmann also argues that time is not merely a concept limiting the nature of man and creation. He also says that God himself is not timeless. The eternity of God is said to be nothing less than endless time and, in some way, our time is a limited part of it.[10] This position erases the boundary between God and man. "God, together with us, is subject to the god, 'Time,' who surrounds both him and us" (cf. Ex. 3:14; John 8:58). This failure to understand the eternity of God may also explain Cullmann's failure to defend the preexistence of Christ in his other books.

---

10. Oscar Cullmann, *Christ and Time* (Philadelphia: The Westminster Press, 1951), p. 62.

Chapter VII

THEOLOGY OF SECULARIZATION

One of the great trends of thought in the West in the twentieth century is the secularization of society. Especially in the last ten years, that trend has begun to influence overtly even theology itself. Until recently, secularists have retained some mild form of innocuous religion. As one evangelical Christian has put it, "they have been afraid to oppose the love and worship of God, even though they have been convinced that the very idea of God is obsolete."

However, even this concessive spirit is rapidly changing. In view of its more recent, radical direction, one commentator has predicted that "by the end of the century, committed Christians will be a conscious minority in the west, surrounded by a militant and arrogant paganism, which is the logical development of our secularist trend."

One of the boldest new displays of apostate man's "secularist flight from God" appears in what many are coming to call "the theology of secularization." A movement with many extremes, it defies definition but demands attention. The well-known "death-of-God movement" may be said to have died as a theological fad. But, as a branch of the secularist theology, it may continue to have an influence in the church far beyond its esoteric teachings. Another advocate behind this new theological direction is Dr. John Robinson, whose best-seller, *Honest to God*,[1] helped to re-

---

1. John Robinson, *Honest to God* (Philadelphia: The Westminster Press, 1963).

vive the new radicalism. Robinson's work starts with the conviction that the idea of God "up there" (whether physically, metaphysically, or metaphorically) is outdated, meaningless, and wrong. Twentieth century theology must have a new "image of God" and a radical reinterpretation of Christian doctrine. God, said Robinson, using the language of Tillich, is "the Ground of our very being," and the church of God was never intended to be an organization for religious men. The motto for believers in the new Christianity must be, "Love God and do what you like." The line between church and world must be erased, he says.

One feels these same demands of secular theology in the book of Harvey Cox, *The Secular City* (1965). Cox's book sought to show that secularization was not the enemy of the gospel but the fruit of the gospel. By secularization, Cox means the historical process by which societies are delivered from church control and closed metaphysical systems. The center of interest in Cox's secularization is the world, not the church or some supernatural realm. In the same spirit, Cox insists we must redefine the God of the Bible as the God of this world, not a God in some fenced-off religious sphere.

These demands by such men as Cox and Robinson are no longer simply a tragic indication of Western capitulation to a secular world. The capitulation is worldwide, a real part of our global-village church. So, C. H. Hwang, formerly of the Tainan Theological College (Presbyterian) in Taiwan, repudiates the theological education pattern imported by the missions as "church directed" and says "we must find a new pattern appropriate and fit for a world-directed missionary community."[2] Prof. Masao Takenaka of Doshisha University, in the John Mott lectures before the East Asia Christian Conference (November, 1961), can speak

---

2. C. H. Hwang, "A Rethinking of Theological Training for the Ministry in the Younger Churches Today," *South East Asia Journal of Theology* IV, 2 (Oct., 1962), 20-21.

of "a new style of Christian life in Asia today" in terms of the new man in Christ "open to secular engagement."[3] Dr. Harold Hong, president of the Methodist Theological Seminary, Seoul, Korea, can tell us that the question of whether we may speak of "the secularization of Christianity" has passed. "Now the only question that remains is how we shall witness about Christ in this secularism. For today's Christian this is an urgent, very immediate and serious task."[4] As in Korea today, the world church's agenda has given top priority to the theology of secularization.[5]

While we therefore recognize the sharp disunity within this general spirit (can we call it a movement?), nevertheless we can recognize several common refrains in the singers of this theological rock music.

1. Secular theologians agree that the problems of this world should be a chief concern for the Christian. They deplore the many ways in which the church has rationalized its failures to confront social and political evils. In this connection, the loudest voice for this participation comes from Dietrich Bonhoeffer, the German pastor who was executed by the Nazis during World War II for taking part in the plot on the life of Hitler. Bonhoeffer's spirit of activism is the spirit of secular theology. This may be one of the reasons why he has almost become its patron saint. Many of the slogans of the movement come from Bonhoeffer's diary and letters written in prison shortly before his execution.

Bonhoeffer called for a "religionless Christianity," for living before God as if God did not exist. His plea was not directed against prayer or worship or the church. It was basically an attack on the idea that there are any spheres

3. Masao Takenaka, "The First Fruits in Asia: Towards a New Style of Christian Life in Asia Today," *South East Asia Journal of Theology* III, 3 (Jan., 1962), p. 22.
4. Harold Hong, *The Christian in Secularism* (Seoul: Christian Literature Society, 1968), p. 5.
5. Kan Ha-bae, *op. cit.*, pp. 42-43.

in life that do not belong to Christ. "Christ cannot be shut up in the sacred society of the Church."[6]

2. Secular theologians generally agree that even our theology must express this spirit of secularization. Harvey Cox says we must stop talking about old-fashioned ontology (ideas of essence and substance) and start talking about functions, about dynamic activism. In the words of Bishop Robinson, the question, "How can I find a gracious God?" must be replaced by the question, "How can I find a gracious neighbor?"[7] According to the extremest of the secular theologians, Paul Van Buren, God himself is to be left out. Christianity, he says, is to be reconstructed without God. Jesus is to be set forth as the paradigm of human existence.[8]

3. Secular theologians demand that the distinctions between the church and the world be erased. In keeping with this spirit, the theme of the second Assembly of the World Council of Churches (1954) was changed from, "Christ the Hope of the Church and the World," to "Christ the Hope of the World." For the same reason, the New Delhi Assembly of the W.C.C. (1961) removed the word "our" from the phrase, "our Lord Jesus Christ," in the Constitutional Basis. "Our" might appear to be restrictive, to set the church off from the world.[9] The church must participate actively in politics, in revolution. For that is said to be where God is acting today. And, in keeping with this desire, evangelism is given new meaning. It is no longer calling men to repentance for sins and faith in Christ. The new evangelism is political activity, social work among the poor.

---

6. Hordern, *op. cit.*, p. 225.

7. Robinson, *op. cit.*, pp. 45 ff.

8. A popular presentation of these ideas can be found in Ved Mehta, *The New Theologian* (New York: Harper and Row, 1965), pp. 55 ff.

9. Edmund P. Clowney, *The Doctrine of the Church* (Nutley, N. J.: Presbyterian and Reformed Publishing Co., 1969), p. 5.

4. There is an effort at a minimum of supernaturalism in the secular theology. The old-fashioned liberal view of Jesus as the perfect man who lived close to God is revived. Robinson describes Christ as "a window into God at work."[10] The atonement then becomes merely Jesus' "utter self-surrender to others in love" in which "he discloses and lays bare the Ground of man's being as Love."[11] So too, secular theologians reject any supernatural kingdom to appear at the second coming of Christ. The only world it knows is the world that is here and now. The idea of heaven is called an "escape hatch" by many.

How does the Calvinist react to the demands of the "secularization of Christianity"? Certainly, we recognize that these men have caught the spirit of our day (we also recognize that they have been caught by the spirit of our day). And, in humility, we must confess that the church has not always been "the light of the world" and "the salt of the earth" (Matt. 5:13-14). Jesus did demand that we be concerned about the evils of our world and seek to correct them (Matt. 25:31-46).

But we cannot feel that the answers of "secular theology" provide the biblical way to be "the salt of the earth."

1. Secular theologians consistently refuse to come to grips with the biblical testimony concerning God, the world, and man. Robinson's ideas, for example, are a caricature of the biblical doctrine of God. Cox's book, *Secular City,* engages in the most dubious exercises in biblical exegesis.

2. Secular theologians, to a greater or lesser degree, have an uncritical admiration for the achievements of modern technology and the mentality of the secular man. The picture of secular man drawn by Paul in Romans 1–3 has no place in their analysis. Secular theology, in its neglect of the reality of sin in modern man's world, is neglecting the awful twist in this world which releases the power of the

10. Robinson, *op. cit.*, p. 71.
11. *Ibid.*, p. 74.

atom and then uses that knowledge to create a bomb, which masters techniques of mass communication and then uses that mastery to develop efficient ways of murdering millions of Jews in Nazi gas chambers.

3. Secular theologians, in their post-Kantian antagonism against metaphysics and ontology, evaporate the distinctive "marks" of the church. The church no longer has an essence as the people of God, elect in Christ, called to be separate from the world (II Cor. 6:14-18). It is redefined in Barthian terminology as exclusively a function—service in the world, service to the world. It ignores the fact that God elects His people to a position as well as a ministry, to status as well as to service (Ex. 15:13, 16; Deut. 32:9). God's love chooses His son, not merely His servant.

4. Secular theologians, in their reinterpretation of Christianity, consistently reject any idea of biblical eschatology rooted in a coming kingdom. The only real kingdom these men recognize is what is present now. And, though Calvinists also believe that in Christ the kingdom is present now (Matt. 12:28; Luke 17:21), its ultimate meaning is future, and its center is always God, not man.[12] The kingdom of heaven will not be perfectly realized until the division between the good and the evil at the consummation of the present age (Matt. 13:47-50).

5. Behind all these shifts and reinterpretations is a basically man-centered approach to the New Testament, strongly dependent on the same Enlightenment mind-set that forms the groundwork for the structuring of men like Barth, Bultmann, and Cullmann.[13] It is a mind-set which cannot therefore, by its very nature, do justice to the God-

---

12. A fully biblical statement of these positions in detail can be found in Geerhardus Vos, *The Teaching of Jesus Concerning the Kingdom of God and the Church* (Philadelphia: Presbyterian and Reformed Publishing Co., 1972), and Herman Ridderbos, *The Coming of the Kingdom* (Philadelphia: Presbyterian and Reformed, 1962).

13. Cornelius Van Til, *Is God Dead?* (Philadelphia: Presbyterian and Reformed Publishing Co., 1966), pp. 31 ff.

centered and Christ-centered emphasis of the Bible. Secular theology speaks of a kingdom centered in the work and future of autonomous man. The only kingdom the Bible knows is centered in the person and work of Christ, never man (Matt. 11:11 ff.; 12:22 ff.). Similarly, the only kingdom work the Bible knows is done, not by man, but by God (Mark 4:26-29).

Secular theology at least indicates what one man has called "a hunger for the re-statement of Christianity in terms that will stand up in the light of modern thought and which can only be translated into terms which are relevant to the twentieth century."[14] There is only one answer for this hunger—a fresh restatement of the doctrines of sovereign grace for a world in love with itself.

14. C. Brown, *op. cit.*, p. 221.

Chapter VIII

SITUATION ETHICS

In the post-Christian situation that marks the Western world, traditional views of Christian ethics are rapidly being abandoned by many. As one American secular magazine writes, "We are witnessing the death of the old morality."[1] One testimony to this decay of biblically oriented standards of ethics is what has been called "situation ethics" or "the new morality."

With roots deep in the ethical principles of men like Barth and Bultmann and Tillich, with theological principles more existential than Puritan, more neo-orthodox than orthodox, the movement exploded most effectively into public notice with the appearance of Bishop John Robinson's book, *Honest to God*, in 1963. Perhaps its most attention-getting form came in 1966 when Joseph Fletcher, professor of social ethics at the Episcopal Seminary, Cambridge, Massachusetts, U.S.A., published his best-seller, *Situation Ethics*.

"Explosion" remains perhaps the best way to describe the way in which the world has received the popularization of these concepts. One commentator has remarked that within a few weeks of the publication of Robinson's *Honest to God*, "a number of translators were at work on editions for Germany, Sweden, Denmark and the Nether-

---

1. Robert Moskin, "Morality USA," *Look*, Sept. 24., 1963, p. 74.

lands."[2] Likely, the history of its appearance in other languages may parallel its publication in Korean in 1968. Within two years four editions had been published, making it one of the ten most popular religious titles in that country in the last 50 years. Two years after its initial runoff, the English language edition had sold 350,000 copies, and the combined world sales had almost touched a million, "which will probably stand as a record in the history of the world for some time to come."[3]

The worldwide popularity of "situation ethics" can hardly be interpreted in countries like Japan and Korea as a manifestation of the third world's "post-Christian mind." Christianity has not been in this part of the world long enough to have reached that stage. But it most certainly can be interpreted as a reflection of the world's acceptance of the presuppositions behind situation ethics. Fletcher has defined those presuppositions as pragmatism (a strategy which holds that a thing is correct or right if it works); relativism (love is the constant and all else variable); positivism (faith propositions are affirmed voluntaristically and not rationalistically); and personalism (people and not things are at the center of concern).[4] He could very well be describing the academic mind of the Far East, in its growing protest against the legalism and binding constrictions of Confucianism, and in its search for new values in a secular society.

Though situation ethics has received most of its adverse attention because of the permissiveness of its sex codes, it is in its broader principles where we must seek to find its central argument.

1. Situation ethics contrasts itself with "traditional ethics" in many ways. It calls itself a reaction against the old morality of laws, rules, and moral principles as guides to

---

2. Ved Mehta, *op. cit.*, p. 3.
3. *Loc. cit.*
4. Joseph Fletcher, *Situation Ethics* (Philadelphia: The Westminster Press, 1966), pp. 40 ff.

conduct. Robinson says that the old morality is deductive, beginning with absolute standards, eternally valid, remaining unchanged. The new morality is said to be inductive, beginning with persons, to emphasize "the priority of persons over principles."[5] The old morality proceeded from the general to the particular, the new morality proceeds from the particular to the general. Robinson assaults traditional Christian ethics as tending to be anti-humanist, oriented to supernatural principles which sometimes take precedence over persons, and to which they must conform regardless of the circumstances.

2. As its name indicates, the new morality emphasizes "the situation," or what contemporary philosophers might call "the existential reality." An act is said to be wrong, not by principle, but by situation. In Robinson's words, "nothing can of itself always be labelled as 'wrong.' One cannot, for instance, start from a position, 'sex relations before marriage' or 'divorce' are wrong in themselves. They may be in 99 cases or even 100 cases out of a 100, but they are not intrinsically so, for the only intrinsic evil is lack of love."[6] According to this view, Christian ethics is not an unchanging body of fixed teaching. Such a view is said to be inherently legalistic and impersonal.

3. The ultimate and only criterion of conduct is said to be not an ethical code, but selfless and sacrificial agape love. This love is to be modelled after Jesus, whom Robinson calls (borrowing the language of Bonhoeffer) "the man for others." The only intrinsic evil for Robinson and Fletcher is lack of love. The only intrinsic good is love, "nothing else at all."[7] Love is to be the ultimate norm of Christian decision, the only norm of conduct.

4. This agape love wills the neighbor's good, whether we like him or not. Love is not an emotional or sentimental ethic. It is an ethic of attitude, of will, and therefore it can

5. Robinson, *op. cit.*, p. 105 ff.
6. *Ibid.*, p. 118.   7. Fletcher, *op. cit.*, p. 69.

be commanded. In the language of Robinson, "love alone, because, as it were, it has a built-in moral compass, enabling it to 'home' intuitively upon the deepest need of the other, can allow itself to be directed completely by the situation."[8]

5. Classic Christian ethics declares that the end does not justify the means. In contrast, Dr. Fletcher says, "only the end justifies the means."[9] Unless justified by some end in view, any action is meaningless. Does an evil means always nullify a good end? No, says situation ethics. Again, it all depends upon the situation in this world of relativities. For example, "if the emotional and spiritual welfare of both parents and children in a particular family can best be served by a divorce, then love requires it."[10]

Certainly, some of the emphases of situation ethics, in a modified sense, resemble biblical Christianity. With Paul, we must warn against the dangers of legalism (Gal. 4:8-10; Col. 2:20-23). With John, we plead the importance of love (I John 4:7, 11, 12, 21). With Jesus, we deplore the mind of the Pharisees, which felt that people were made for rules and not rules for people (Mark 2:27-28). We suspect that part of the reason for the warm reception of situation ethics in Asia may be the reaction of young people to the legalism and rule-centered ethic of Confucianism which has bound society there together for so long. Nevertheless, the Christian who is willing to subject his ethical life to the rule of the sovereign Christ will have radical difficulties with the arguments of the new morality. Using some of the guidelines for criticism provided by Carl Henry, we would indicate some of these difficulties.

1. By freeing moral decision from the authority of divine commandments and objective moral principle, the new morality continually threatens to debase agape into eros. Love's content is the law and cannot be separated from that

---

8. Robinson, *op. cit.*, p. 115.
9. Fletcher, *op. cit.*, p. 120.   10. *Ibid.*, p. 133.

content without destroying its very character as love. As Paul indicates, love for neighbor is reflected by the law. "The commandments, 'You shall not commit adultery, You shall not kill, You shall not steal, You shall not covet,' and any other commandment, are summed up in this sentence, 'You shall love your neighbor as yourself.' Love does no wrong to a neighbor; therefore love is the fulfillment of the law" (Rom. 13:9-10).[11]

2. "By narrowing ethical duty to moment-by-moment confrontation and response, the new morality thwarts the Christian requirement of a consistent, predictable pattern of life.

3. By tapering the whole of moral duty to agape love, the new morality fails to reflect the individual's answerability to justice in public affairs and accordingly sponsors a highly subjective approach to social ethics.

4. By detaching the entire teaching of the Bible from the revelation of the sovereign moral Lord of the universe, and demeaning that teaching to the level of a revisable guideline, and by regarding agape love alone as the fixed content of ethical life, the new morality falls under the judgment of the very Scriptures it apparently honors in its partial and restricted appeals to the Bible. The fact that now and then its advocates invoke the Bible should confer no scriptural dignity upon the new morality. Instead, it bestows upon the Bible this tribute, that even at a distance of twenty centuries those who promote a new morality are not wholly able to dissociate themselves from remnants of its influence."[12]

5. The new morality detaches ethical theory from the supernatural Creator and Redeemer of Scripture. Robinson builds his system by rejecting God as a supreme, personal, supernatural being, independent of the world. In line with

---

11. Henlee Barnett, *The New Theology and Morality* (Philadelphia: The Westminster Press, 1967), pp. 44-45.

12. Carl F. H. Henry, *Faith at the Frontiers* (Chicago: Moody Press, 1969), p. 142.

Tillich's speculations, Robinson contends that all language about what he calls the Ultimate is symbolical and relative. God is no longer the sovereign Distinguisher of right and wrong, but is merely "the Ground of all Being." This God of situation ethics is too small, too restricted to provide an adequate dynamic for His love ethic. Thusly, the new morality predicates the case for love on mythological supports and supplies no firm basis for ethics.

6. The new morality reconstructs the Jesus of the Bible by expressly repudiating the gospel testimony that Jesus gave commandments to His disciples and that Jesus viewed obedience to these commandments as a test of their personal love to Him (John 15:8-10, 14). By doing this, the new morality forfeits its right to expound authentically Christian ethics.

7. Situation ethics is built on an apostate view of human nature and human sin. They assume that "love has a built-in moral compass" so unaffected by man's sin and corruption that it will intuitively make proper choices. This is a far cry from what Paul says about man's "moral compass" in Romans 1:18-32 or Romans 3:10-18. Love, directed by the human heart, cannot make either wise choices or choices directed to the welfare of others (Matt. 15:19). Its choices are always self-centered. Martin Luther once said that "reason is a whore." So is love, without redeeming grace.

8. Situation ethics constructs its program without any attention to repentance, judgment, faith, and redemption. As one man has noted, Robinson leaves the impression that modern man is so grown up that he has little need now for spiritual help outside of his own natural resources. This author suspects that this noticeable lack may explain the wide attention given to the theories of situation ethics in non-Christian circles in the West and in Asia. Situation ethics asks for nothing by way of ethics and it assumes nothing by way of theology. What better system for "the natural man" than this?

58

Chapter IX

THEOLOGY OF HOPE

In 1965, in the summer heat of the "death-of-God" movement, amidst what some feared might become a revival of Christian atheism, a new note was sounded in Germany by a young theology professor at Tubingen University. Although it is quite early even to speak of a new movement of theology, the title and topic of Jurgen Moltmann's (1926–) book, *The Theology of Hope*, already have struck the nerve endings of the academic world.

Already other names are mentioned in connection with the emphasis of Moltmann—Wolfhart Pannenberg of Munich, Ernst Benz of Marburg. Some consider the former as the systematic theologian of the movement,[1] the latter as the historian. Though this writer prefers to regard Pannenberg as part of another movement (see the following chapter), it is still true that these men share enough common emphases to indicate some possible collaboration in the future toward the rise of an embryonic common school of thought.[2]

The United States has already given enough attention to Moltmann's ideas to insure future discussion for some time. Moltmann's book appeared in English only two years after

1. Aaron P. Park, "The Christian Hope According to Bultmann, Pannenberg and Moltmann," *Westminster Theological Journal* XXXIII, 2 (May, 1971), 153 ff.

2. David P. Scaer, "Jurgen Moltmann and His Theology of Hope," *Journal of the Evangelical Theological Society* XIII, 2 (Spring, 1970), 69 ff.

its initial publication in German, a rather accelerated rate for most translated works. And, among American theologians, Dr. Carl Braaten, a rising young scholar of the Lutheran Church, seems to be aligning himself with Moltmann's emphases.[3] This may indicate the beginnings of an American movement. The strongly optimistic, and cultural note of the "theology of hope" will likely prove much more attractive to American theologians than the pessimistic discords of men like Altizer and Van Buren.

There is every reason to believe that, for many of these same reasons, "the theology of hope" can be expected to receive a wide hearing in Asia as well. Dr. Hideo Ohki of the Tokyo Union Theological Seminary has already been deeply impressed by Moltmann's analysis of the twentieth century as, not promethean, but sisyphean. "His hopes ruined again and again, modern man huddles in the midst of history without ideals and without God."[4] Moltmann's call to hope "thus becomes a burning question."[5] In Korea, 1969–1970 saw two of Moltmann's titles already in translation.[6]

Since Moltmann's 1967 title, *The Theology of Hope*, first appeared, a second volume has also been published in English translation, *Religion, Revolution and the Future* (1969). In this second work, Moltmann emphasizes what he feels are the ethical and practical implications of his earlier work. While many critics felt the first work was a refreshing call for a deeper appreciation of eschatology in Christian theology, and a blistering attack on existential theologians like Bultmann, the second goes far in underlining the reasons

---

3. Carl Braaten, *History and Hermeneutics* (Philadelphia: The Westminster Press, 1966), pp. 177-179; Carl Braaten, *The Future of God* (New York: Harper and Row, 1969).
4. Hideo Ohki, "Democracy, Eschatology and Ecstasy," *Northeast Asia Journal of Theology* (March, 1970), 16.
5. *Ibid.*, 17.
6. The two titles were, *Herrschaft Christi und Sociale Wirklichkeit nach Dietrich Bonhoeffer* (1959), and *Perspektiven der Theologie* (1968).

for the orthodox theologian's earlier reluctance to greet Moltmann's first book with unreserved praise. For while Moltmann blames the form critics for dissolving history into what they call "the existential moment of faith," he himself dissolves history into the future (in his first book) and the future into revolution (in his second book).

1. The key to understanding Moltmann's "futuristic theology" is his idea that God is subject to the process of time. In this process, God is not fully God, because God is part of time which is pushing forward into the future. In traditional Christianity, God and Jesus Christ stand, first of all, outside of time. In Moltmann's theology, eternity is lost in time. According to Moltmann, the God of the Bible is a God with "future as his essential nature."[7] God does not reveal who He is, but rather who He will be in the future. God is present only in His promises, only in hope. According to Moltmann, we can make only functional statements about the God of hope. Our God will be God when He fulfills His promises and thus establishes His reign. God is not the absolute. He is the God of faithfulness who makes promises about the future and is, himself, determined by the future.

2. According to Moltmann, all Christian theology must be molded and shaped by eschatology. But what is eschatology? It is not the traditional anticipation of the second coming of Christ. It is interpreted by Moltmann as openness toward the future, the freedom of the future. There is no supernatural sphere where God already exists in eternity. There is no fixed moment when time shall come to an end. The future is an unknown quantity to both man and God.

3. The evangelical Christian closely relates the resurrection of Christ to eschatology. The risen Christ is "the first fruits of the resurrection" (I Cor. 15:23; Acts 4:2). The death and resurrection of Christ are God's guarantee of the

7. Jurgen Moltmann, *The Theology of Hope* (New York: Harper and Row, 1967), pp. 29-32, 42 ff.

coming resurrection, the beginning of the final resurrection, a historical fact that gives meaning to our future.[8] However, to Moltmann, the question of the historicity of the bodily resurrection of Jesus is not valid. Did Jesus Christ rise from the dead 1900 years ago with his physical body? Moltmann says that that is an irrelevant question. We must not look from Calvary to the new Jerusalem, he says. Rather, we must look from our unlimited future back to Calvary. Traditionally, it is stated that Christ's resurrection is the historical basis of the final resurrection. Moltmann would say that the final resurrection is the basis of Jesus' resurrection.[9] Rather than standing at the open tomb and looking forward, we are to project ourselves into the final resurrection.

4. But man must not wait for his future passively. He must participate actively in society. The task of the church is to preach in such a way that, in the present, the future grasps the individual and thrusts him into definitive action to shape the future.[10] The purpose of the church is not so much "to report on the past as to change the future. The present in itself is not important. What is important is that in the present, the future grasps the individual. . . ." Man must become aware of his messianic possibilities.

5. To realize the future in society, the categories of the past in society must be discarded. According to Moltmann, there are no fixed forms or structures in the world, given by God at creation. In direct opposition to the traditional Christian position, Moltmann asserts that God has not laid down authoritarian forms which are to be used in realizing the future. Future means freedom and freedom means relativity.[11]

---

8. An excellent contribution to the study of these themes may be found in Richard B. Gaffin, Jr., *Resurrection and Redemption: A Study in Pauline Soteriology* (mimeographed by Westminster Student Service, Westminster Theological Seminary, 1971).

9. Jurgen Moltmann, *Religion, Revolution and the Future* (New York: Charles Scribner's Sons, 1969), p. 52.

10. *Ibid.*, pp. 118 ff.

11. *Ibid.*, p. 138.

6. The church's purpose is to be the instrument through which God will bring about universal, social reconciliation. As one commentator has noted regarding Moltmann, "the kingdom of grace merges into the universal kingdom of power."[12] This participation of the church in society may use revolution as an appropriate means, but not necessarily the only one. And, in this revolutionary push toward the future, "the problem of violence and non-violence" is called "an illusory problem. There is only the question of the justified and unjustified use of force and the question of whether the means are proportionate to the ends."[13]

As in the "secular theology" movement, one recognizes here too a deep awareness of the responsibility of the church for the world. The Calvinist can also sympathize with Moltmann's desire to look at the Bible from beginning to end as an eschatological book. We have often been too guilty of hiding our eschatology in the back of our books on systematic theology and not infusing our daily life with its perspective. It is a ringing call for action now (II Peter 3:10-11).

But every conservative will also recognize the glaring errors in Moltmann and the horrors which his view of ethics might conceivably unfold.

1. Though Moltmann is critical of many of the neo-orthodox concepts,[14] he works from the presupposition that "theology of the word" is the only "appropriate" designation for dialectic theology.[15] In fact, as Braaten has argued, he carries Barthian principles even further.[16] Barth had transcendentalized eschatology through his use of the *Historie-Geschichte* dialectic. Moltmann has simply carried this polemic against an objective realm of history one step

---

12. David Scaer, *op. cit.*, p. 76.
13. Moltmann, *op. cit.*, p. 143.
14. Moltmann, *Theology of Hope, op. cit.*, pp. 39 ff., 50 ff.
15. Quoted in James M. Robinson and John B. Cobb, Jr., *Theology as History* (New York: Harper and Row, 1967), p. 17.
16. Carl Braaten, *History and Hermeneutics, op. cit.*, p. 178.

further, now rejecting even the "already" of *Historie* for a view of history swallowed up by the "not yet." If Barth's presuppositions tore away the possibility of any real correlation between history and faith, Moltmann's have torn away even the possibility of history itself. The Kantian dialectic which Moltmann rebels against in Barth has turned upon itself.[17]

2. Though Moltmann drapes his theology in biblical idioms of "eschatology" and "resurrection" and "consummation," his system is far more indebted to Marxism than to Christ. And here again, the congeniality of the notion of dialectic, which forms the heart of Marxism, would find points of contact with the dialectic concept of truth forming Moltmann's new twists on neo-orthodoxy. So, Moltmann's first book is an exercise in dialogue with the German atheistic Marxist, Ernst Bloch. And his second work makes it abundantly clear that the "dialogue" has obviously been a two-way one. In the exchange, Moltman may have learned as much as Bloch.

3. Moltmann's view of eschatology loses its biblical center. That center is the coming of God in Christ to save His people. When Jesus died and rose again nineteen hundred years ago, the "last days" began (Acts 2:17; Heb. 1:2; I John 2:18). One day, when Jesus returns on the clouds of glory, the consummation of the last days will take place. But one does not find Jesus Christ at the center of Moltmann's eschatology. It is a man-centered system, man looking toward the future. In that sense, critics have wisely indicated that Moltmann's ideas might better be called "futurology" rather than "eschatology." The goal of Moltmann's future is not the full manifestation of Christ's glory, but the building of Utopia on earth.

4. To Moltmann, the kingdom of God is ushered in by politics and revolution. To the apostle Paul, the kingdom

---

17. Van Til, *The Great Debate Today, op. cit.,* pp. 202-204.

of God is, and will be, ushered in by the proclamation of the saving power of Jesus Christ (Acts 28:30-31). To Moltmann, that kingdom is a tangible earthly reality. To Christ, it can be entered into only by faith in Him (John 3:3, 5). And it brings peace, not revolution (Rom. 14:17).

5. Because Moltmann builds on the philosophical axiom that time is the substance of reality, he must rebuild God himself to fit that narrow concept of reality. The future becomes not merely an unknown quantity to man. It becomes also an unknown quantity to God. God, according to Moltmann, no longer exists from eternity to eternity. He exists only in the future, propelled along by the movement of time. At Mount Sinai, God said to Moses, "I am that I am." Moltmann will not let God say that to him.

CHAPTER X

THEOLOGY OF HISTORY

In the late 1950's, what many have felt to be a new theological emphasis began to be heard in the theological journals of Germany. The emphasis could be seen in the doctoral theses of such new young scholars as Ulrich Wilckens (now professor of New Testament in Berlin), Rolf Rendtorff (now professor of Old Testament at the University of Heidelberg), and Klaus Koch (now teaching Old Testament at the University of Hamburg). But the center of the new circle, and the man who gives it its most systematic form, is the young professor of systematic theology at the University of Mainz, Wolfhart Pannenberg (1928–). Referred to in its initial stages as "the Pannenberg circle," it has increasingly been called "the theology of history" or the "theology of resurrection."

There are still those who associate this circle closely with the work of Moltmann and the emerging "theology of hope" emphasis. Certainly, Pannenberg and Moltmann share many concerns in common—a renewed interest in the relation of history and faith; a desire to orient theology to the future and, in particular, to the resurrection of Christ; a strong attempt to break away from the existentialist emphases of Bultmann. But, although these men have written little about one another's arguments,[1] it may be premature to place them in the same school of thought. For, while there

---

1. Moltmann, *op. cit.*, p. 76-84.

are areas of agreement, there are also some sharp differences. Moltmann is, by no means, as interested as Pannenberg in grounding faith in history. Faith, according to Pannenberg, relates itself to the past. According to Moltmann, faith relates itself to the future, not to the God who said, but to the God who will say. In this sense, Moltmann is still more deeply tied to Bultmann than to Pannenberg. Both speak of the centrality of the resurrection for the Christian faith. But Moltmann disavows any interest in a bodily resurrection as "irrelevant," whereas Pannenberg recognizes the historical reality of the resurrection as crucial to New Testament Christianity. It would also appear that Pannenberg does not share Moltmann's more recent emphasis on the relation between eschatology and Marxist patterns of social revolution.

1. Like Moltmann, Pannenberg is insisting on a return to the basic question of history and faith. Bultmann's dissolving of history into individual existence is attacked by Pannenberg as an attempt to flee into some suprahistorical harbor supposedly safe from the critical historical flood tide.[2] Not only this, but even Barth is criticized for hiding his theology in the harbor of pre-history.[3] One critic has said that "the theology of history is the first theological school to emerge in Germany within recent years that is not, in one form or another, a development of the dialectical theology of the 1920's." This statement seems inaccurate, but it does indicate Pannenberg's intent to separate himself from the dialectic pattern of *Historie* and *Geschichte*. According to Pannenberg, the claims of Barth and Bultmann for a kerygma without history "is a meaningless noise. The preaching of the 'Word of God' is an empty assertion if it is severed from what really happened. Faith cannot live

---

2. Wolfhart Pannenberg, "Redemptive Event and History," *Essays on Old Testament Hermeneutics*, ed. by Claus Westermann (Richmond: John Knox Press, 1964), pp. 314-315.
3. *Loc. cit.*

67

from a kerygma detached from its historical basis and content."[4] And this, according to Pannenberg, is precisely what Barth and Bultmann do. By severing history from the kerygma, they sever faith's lifeline to truth.

2. Pannenberg insists that God's revelation does not come to man immediately, but always mediately through the events of history. And this history in which revelation takes place is not a special redemptive revelation known only through faith (which is the argument of the *Heilsgeschichte* school). Pannenberg refuses to make any cleavage between salvation history and world history (a common feature of both *Heilsgeschichte* and existentialist views of revelation). There is no direct, special revelation of God, after the fashion of a theophany. According to Pannenberg, there is only indirect revelation through historical acts.

3. Universal history, then, is the exclusive medium for revelation, according to Pannenberg. Not any particular part of history or any strand of history, but history as a whole is God's teacher. Unlike special manifestations of God, historical revelation is available for anyone who has eyes to see. It is universal in character. Historical knowledge provides the sole basis for faith. Faith, then, becomes the knowledge of what is true about history.

4. The meaning of history can be found only at its end, not its center (as Cullmann taught). That end has taken place proleptically in the resurrection of Christ. Because, according to Pannenberg, the resurrection of Christ was the antecedent revelation to the events of the end of the world, the resurrection enables us to grasp the whole of history.[5] It is the key to understanding everything in history. This emphasis has led many to call Pannenberg's thinking a "theology of the resurrection."

---

4. Braaten, *op. cit.*, p. 26.
5. Wolfhart Pannenberg, *Grundzüge der Christologie* (Gerd Mohn: Gutersloher Verlagshaus, 1964), p. 88 ff.

5. Unlike Moltmann, Pannenberg says he seeks to avoid, for the most part, demythologizing the resurrection. He does not hesitate to call it a historical event.[6] He calls himself convinced not only that the church's belief in the resurrection is not prefabricated myth (as Bultmann taught) but also that the resurrection is historically demonstrable (in opposition to the *Heilsgeschichte* school). He refuses to explain the gospel stories of the resurrection wholly as the work of the apostles' imagination. The apostles, he says, were too discouraged after the death of Jesus to have talked themselves into believing that Jesus was risen from the dead. The only satisfactory explanation for their sudden faith was that Jesus appeared to them.[7] Furthermore, the early Christian community could not have survived if the tomb of Jesus had not been empty. An occupied tomb would have destroyed their faith, and given the Jews a strong argument against the church.

There is much in Pannenberg's claims for which the orthodox Christian can be grateful. He has helped to remind the contemporary theological world that there is not much of a gap between Bultmann and Barth. Both refuse to bring Christian faith in relation to the realm of objective knowledge. Both are advocates of a dialectical theology which undermines both historical revelation and the universal validity of Christian truth. Pannenberg properly sees that the neo-orthodox denial of the objectivity of revelation is a threat to the very reality of revelation. We may also be grateful that he is reminding the theological world that the Christian truth is the one truth for all men. In refuting the neo-orthodox notion that the truth of revelation becomes truth only for individuals by personal appropriation, he is stressing the unity of all truth in a way badly needed today. He has also made it excessively difficult for any modern

6. Daniel P. Fuller, *Easter Faith and History* (Grand Rapids: Eerdmans Publishing Co., 1965), pp. 177 ff.
7. Pannenberg, *op. cit.*, pp. 95 f.

critic to retain the Bultmannian skepticism toward the resurrection.

Nevertheless, it would be most unwise to label Pannenberg as a "conservative" or an "evangelical." His system of thought is, by no means, a return to the emphasis of historic, biblical Christianity.

1. Though Pannenberg attacks Barth's and Bultmann's positions on the relation of faith and history, in many respects the Pannenberg group may seem more the heir of neo-orthodoxy than its opponent. Along with neo-orthodoxy, he accepts a view of reality "virtually the same as that which springs from Kant's primacy of the practical reason. It is the view of Renaissance man. . . . There is no transition from wrath to grace in history according to the theology of Pannenberg."[8] Though he condemns the Barthian dialectic in revelation, and insists that revelation is objective in the form of historical events, he retains a dialectic bifurcation by saying revelation is objective in the form of historical events, but not in concepts. "While revelation does take the form of thought, he holds it does not do so authoritatively in the special form of concepts supernaturally given once for all, as in old Protestant theology. The Christian tradition is always in development, he contends, because revelation is given 'in deeds or acts that remain to be explained.' "[9]

2. From this dialectic comes Pannenberg's refusal to identify the whole Bible with revelation. So, along with neo-orthodoxy, he accepts much of the results of negative historical criticism. He insists over and over again that the virgin birth is a myth. He agrees with Bultmann in asserting that the titles expressing Jesus' divinity were created by the early church and read back into the lips of Jesus.

3. His discussion of the resurrection is also not without several major flaws. He does not accept as completely

8. Van Til, *op. cit.*, pp. 201-202.
9. Henry, *op. cit.*, pp. 73-74.

reliable the resurrection narratives. Here too he claims to find inaccuracies and legendary materials in the Gospels. He also asserts that "in all probability the earthly Jesus' expectation was not directed toward . . . a privately experienced resurrection from the dead but toward the imminent universal resurrection of the dead, which would, of course, include himself should his death precede it."[10]

In other words, Jesus mistakenly assumed that His bodily resurrection would coincide with the end of the world and the general resurrection of all believers. According to Pannenberg, as late as twenty to thirty years after the death of Jesus, Paul was still expecting as well this imminent, ultimate arrival of the resurrected Jesus for judgment, accompanied by the universal resurrection of the dead. He claims that one does not find this emphasis in such second-generation writings as the Gospels, because they now realized that the resurrection of Jesus was a special event that happened to Jesus only.

This position of Pannenberg destroys with the left hand what he has built with the right hand. It assumes inherent contradiction between the biblical records concerning the resurrection of Jesus. Even worse, it must assume that Jesus was mistaken about himself and His resurrection. It also ignores the vast testimony in the Gospels and in Paul's letters, which assume a lengthy delay between the time of Christ's resurrection and His second coming in judgment (cf. Matt. 24:42, 50; 25:1-14; Mark 8:38; I Cor. 1:7, 4:5).

4. By making faith exclusively dependent on history that is known through historical research, Pannenberg accepts also the corollary that ordinary people are not capable of believing on their own, but only as they submit themselves to the authority of the learned historian. In doing this, Pannenberg leaves the ultimate step of faith, not in the hands of the simple believer, but the scholarly theologian

10. Wolfhart Pannenberg, *Jesus—God and Man* (Philadelphia: The Westminster Press, 1968), p. 66.

who establishes the trustworthiness of the information.[11]

5. Critics have also indicated that Pannenberg cannot explain satisfactorily, on this basis, the reason for unbelief. If faith is based exclusively on the knowledge of history, does this not break down the antithesis between faith and sight (II Cor. 5:7)? Further, what place is there in the thinking of Pannenberg for "the enlightenment of the Holy Spirit"? If history is the sole foundation for faith, why is it that when Paul preached the resurrection in Athens some believed while others mocked (Acts 17:32-34)? On the premises of Pannenberg, this question becomes impossible to answer.[12]

11. Fuller, *op. cit.*, pp. 183-184.
12. *Ibid.*, pp. 185-186.

CHAPTER XI

THEOLOGY OF EVOLUTION

One of the most interesting religious events of the late
1950's and the mid-1960's has been the posthumous popularity of the Jesuit scientist and mystic, Father Pierre
Teilhard de Chardin (1881–1955). The founder of what
might best be called a "theology of evolution," Teilhard was
forbidden by the hierarchy of the Roman Catholic Church
to publish any books during his lifetime because of their
"heretical contents."

But, within fifteen years of his death, his books, suppressed during his lifetime, have continued to appear. And
his thought continues to shake the world of science and
theology in the West. A professor in Roman Catholic
Fordham University (U.S.A.) predicts Teilhard "will become the church's new philosophical system." In 1963, an
article appeared under the title, "The Priest Who Haunts
the Catholic World," predicting that the outcome of the
Second Vatican Council "will either reflect the Teilhard
spirit or it will accomplish nothing of importance." Twenty-
seven Roman Catholic scholars in 1960 predicted that
"Teilhard's thought may ultimately lead to the most radical
re-dressing of Catholic philosophy since Thomas Aquinas
introduced Aristotle into the medieval church seven centuries ago."

None of this should be interpreted to mean that Teilhard's
influence is strictly in the West or in Catholic theology
exclusively. Some of his most ardent commentators are

Protestant scientists and theologians. And already his thinking has begun to touch the third world, though still in a beginning stage. A young Ecuadorian scholar, Francisco Bravo, recently produced a careful work on Teilhard, which Ivan Illich, executive director of the Center of Intercultural Formation, Mexico, has described as "a prime opportunity for English readers to become aware of the unsuspected importance this author has assumed in a world which is conscious of its own growth yet often called 'underdeveloped.' "[1] Dom Helder Camara, archbishop of Olinda and Recife, Brazil, pays homage to Teilhard for reminding man of the Christ and man's own courage. This, says Illich, "is an example of the repercussions that Teilhardian thought is creating in Latin America today."[2]

In the Far East as well, Teilhard's influence grows. Prof. Suh Nam-dong, dean of the College of Theology, Yonsei University, Seoul, Korea, has taken themes from Teilhard and developed them into a concept of what he calls "the cosmic Christ," the new humanity, the Christ of the future.[3]

Many factors help to explain Teilhard's sudden and immense popularity. His outstanding personality, the humanity of his character, are quickly apparent to anyone who has either read about his life or merely touched the priest's life through his published books.[4] To the scientific world, he appeals as a geologist and paleontologist of high distinction. To mention merely one of his scientific contributions, he took part in the expedition which unearthed the skull of the so-called Peking Man. To the theological world, he appeals as a mystic who has sought to combine the best of the two worlds—evolution and the Roman Catholic

---

1. Francisco Bravo, *Christ in the Thought of Teilhard de Chardin* (Notre Dame: University of Notre Dame Press, 1967), p. vi.
2. *Loc. cit.*
3. Suh Nam-dong, "The Contemporaneous Christ," *Northeast Asia Journal of Theology*, September, 1969, pp. 10-13.
4. Henri De Lubac, *Teilhard de Chardin, The Man and His Meaning* (New York: Hawthorn Books, Inc., 1965), pp. 3-130.

Church. To modern man, he appeals as an adventurer (twenty years spent in China as a scientist), the underdog (forbidden by "the establishment" to publish anything relating to his evolutionary theories), and the man of principle (remaining loyal to his order, in spite of their restrictions on his writing).

1. The starting point of Teilhard's thought is evolution, what he calls "a light illuminating all facts, a curve that all lines must follow."[5] The earth, he says, was formed not less than five and probably not more than ten thousand million years ago. Since that time, its evolutionary process has gone on.

2. This evolutionary process moves according to what he calls "the Law of Complexity Consciousness." That is, there is a tendency in evolution for matter to become increasingly complex . . . elemental particles (the Alpha point) into atoms, atoms into molecules, molecules into living cells, cells into multicellular organisms.[6]

On the other hand, there is a corresponding rise in the consciousness of matter. Teilhard describes this secondary part of the process in terms of "spheres," language long popular with the scientist in describing the earth. The earliest stages of evolution are designated the "barysphere" (the time of the molten interior of the earth). This is followed in time by the "lithosphere" (the time of the forming of the hard crust on the earth). Then comes the "hydrosphere" (the water in the sea and the air), and the "atmosphere" (the development of the gaseous envelope surrounding the earth).[7]

At this point in the evolutionary history of the earth, according to Teilhard, biological life appears on the earth.

---

5. Teilhard de Chardin, *The Phenomenon of Man* (New York: Harper and Row, 1961), p. 241.
6. John Macquarrie, *Twentieth-Century Religious Thought* (New York: Harper and Row, 1963), pp. 271-272.
7. Teilhard, *op. cit.*, pp. 328-330.

The word "biosphere" is used to denote this living layer of creatures which had evolved out of the other layers. To describe the next stage, Teilhard, in 1920, invented a new word, "noosphere."[8] He used it to denote the next step in evolution, the formation of a "mind layer" on the earth, the appearance of thinking man on the earth. The stage is one of the most important in the history of the world, according to him. He also calls it "hominization." At this stage, the evolutionary process becomes conscious of itself, and man becomes a spearhead.

3. At this stage in his evolutionary theory, Teilhard draws in theology by predicting the evolutionary future. He sees the whole evolutionary process beginning from elemental particles (the Alpha point) and converging upon what he calls "the Omega point," that is, a suprapersonal unity of all things in God.[9] In this view, God becomes the final rather than the efficient cause of all the universe, drawing all things toward perfection in himself. This is the stage, he says, when God will be "all in all" (I Cor. 15:28), "a superior form of pantheism," "the expectation of perfect unity, steeped in which each element will reach its consummation at the same time as the universe."[10]

4. The center of this evolutionary process, its inner principle, is said to be Christ. The Christ of Teilhard, as one commentator has noted, "is the reflection into the heart of the process of the Omega point which stands at its end. Christ assures us of its reality by actualizing it in our midst. . . ." By a personal act of communion and sublimation, Christ aggregates to himself the total psychism of the earth. The universe fulfills itself in Christ in a synthesis of centers in perfect conformity with the laws of union.

5. This moving towards the Christ-center, the Omega point, is the process of love. Love, says Teilhard, is not

---

8. *Ibid.*, pp. 200-204.
9. *Ibid.*, p. 322.
10. *Loc. cit.*

peculiar to man, but the general property of all life, that is to say, the affinity of being with being. Driven by the forces of love, the fragments of the world seek each other so that the world may come to being.

Teilhard's principles offer many difficulties for a sympathetic appraisal by the Calvinist. His language is torturous. His effort to make Christ the key to evolution seems inherently contradictory to most of us. But, to his credit, he reminds us that we must take science seriously as Christians, and he has apparently reminded the materialists of science that this world is not simply governed by blind, purposeless determinism. If his system cannot be accepted, it should at least succeed in stimulating the biblically oriented Christian to develop a better one—one that will do biblical justice to the world as a manifestation of God's plan and the cosmic dimensions of God's salvation (Rom. 8:19-22).

As a theology of evolution, Teilhard's system fails to provide us with that orientation.

1. The root error in Teilhard's program is the dichotomy of nature and grace that marks Thomistic thought generally and his in particular. For each part of the dichotomy there is a separate source of revelation, in the natural sphere an autonomous human reason "which is supposed to be capable of discovering the natural truths by its own light. *The Phenomenon of Man* reflects, in fact, a philosophical attempt of autonomous human reason to discover the substance of the Deity, and His supreme intentions, in 'nature.' "[11] For the world of grace, the divine Word is the source of revelation. And one can see its influence in Teilhard's book, *The Divine Milieu*, where it undergirds the presentation of a theology of revelation. This dichotomy, incompatible with the central motives of the Christian faith, is "presented anew in a modernized fashion by Teilhard de Chardin by accommodating it to the humanistic ideal of free personality which, since

11. J. J. Duyvene De Wit, "Pierre Teilhard de Chardin," *Creative Minds in Contemporary Theology, op. cit.*, p. 437.

Kant, expresses itself in the dualistically opposed religious basic motives of nature and freedom."[12]

2. From this root in synthesis comes the rest of Teilhard's divergencies with biblical truth. Like other evolutionary theories, Teilhard's defense of evolution still remains explicitly at variance with the Bible's description of the origin of life through the fiat creation of God (Gen. 1). Many contemporary evangelical theologians concede the vast antiquity of the earth, and the possibility of the development of a wide variety of species from the specially created "kinds" of life (Gen. 1:21, 24, 25).[13] But none of these concessions are felt to be weakening the biblical revelation of creation. They are merely a recognition of the role of natural revelation in the interpretation of special revelation. Teilhard's theory completely neglects the most obvious emphasis of Scripture—the work of creation as "God's making all things of nothing, by the word of His power, in the space of six days, and all very good."[14]

3. Like other evolutionary theories, Teilhard's ideas also assume that man reaches his true dignity and spiritual fulfillment through the evolutionary process. This is contrary to the revelations of grace. "For Christian theology, there is only one such perfect man, Jesus Christ. And man can attain his true destiny only in and through his relation to Jesus Christ."[15]

4. Like other evolutionary theories, Teilhard's ideas also predicate the understanding of evolution as what he calls

---

12. *Ibid.*, p. 438. For a full critique along these lines, consult Cornelius Van Til, *Teilhard de Chardin: Evolution and Christ* (Philadelphia: Presbyterian and Reformed Publishing Co., 1966).

13. Bolton Davidheiser, *Evolution and Christian Faith* (Nutley. N. J.: Presbyterian and Reformed Publishing Co., 1969); Bernard Ramm, *Christian View of Science and Scripture* (Grand Rapids: Eerdmans Publishing Co., 1955).

14. *Westminster Shorter Catechism*, Q. 9.

15. R. Hooykaas, "Teilhardism, a Pseudo-scientific Delusion." *Free University Quarterly* IX (1963), 1-57.

"the most prodigious event perhaps ever recorded by history." As a Dutch Calvinist has said, "Teilhard becomes so excited about evolution that he even forgets that, according to his Christian belief, the greatest event in history is the coming of Jesus Christ, and not the discovery of evolution."[16]

5. Like other evolutionary theories, Teilhard's "theology of evolution" is overly optimistic. He promises an optimistic end for all of us without any reference to the gracious activity of God. This may be one reason for its rapid spread. Modern man is willing to swallow any kind of opiate if it is presented to him in the name of science.

6. In this same connection, just as Teilhard's views do not allow God's grace to be grace, so also he does not allow man's sin to be sin. Teilhard's unfaltering proclamation of the harmony and unity of the whole creation is never broken by the biblical reality of man's sin and its effects on that harmony. For this reason, the biblical theme of judgment hardly appears in Teilhard's universe. "In Teilhard, evil emerges as a sort of superabundance from the very structure of evolving world itself. It manifests itself on different planes, for example as material disorder, or as decomposition resulting from unhappy chance; as death which is an indispensable condition of the replacement of one individual by another along a phyletic stem; as solitude and anxiety accompanying the labor pains of a consciousness wakening up to reflection; or as growth, with all its risks and all its painful efforts to progress in the direction of the highest synthesis of the spirit. Here again, we recognize the disastrous influence of early scholasticism which aimed at an accommodation of Greek thought to the doctrines of the Christian faith."[17]

---

16. *Ibid.*, pp. 58-83. Compare also, D. Gareth Jones, *Teilhard de Chardin: An Analysis and Assessment* (Downers Grove, Ill.: Inter-Varsity Press, 1970), pp. 64 ff.

17. Duyvene De Wit, *op. cit.*, p. 444.

7. Teilhard's view that the universe represents the still-becoming organical body of Christ produces at least two major deficiencies: the deification of the functional, organic creation; and the mythical transformation of the Christ of the Bible into some mystical, cosmic Christ. In the end, we lose both the world and Jesus Christ.

CHAPTER XII

PROCESS THEOLOGY

In the last ten years of Western theology, increasingly one issue has kept reappearing for discussion—the doctrine of God. In recent years, a deluge of books has appeared on this subject.[1] Many factors explain the rise of this issue. In the philosophical world, what has been called "analytical philosophy" has raised the question whether it is even possible to talk intelligently about God.[2] It continues to ask if even language about God can be meaningful. As we have noted in an earlier chapter, the various strains of secular theology are demanding that we speak about God in a secular way, that we erase the metaphysical dividing line between the Creator and the creature, between God and the world. The faddistic "God-is-dead" theology has even asked whether God himself is real or not. Tillich and his popularizer, Bishop John Robinson, point up the problems in connection with thinking of God as "up there" and suggest we think of God as being in the depths of life, the Ground of our being.

In this situation, one group of theologians has arisen to try to reestablish the doctrine of God in a skeptical world. Largely American in origin, this new shift, called "process theology," seems to have been associated with the University of Chicago, and one of its professors, Dr. Charles Hart-

---

1. C. Brown, *op. cit.*, pp. 305-306.
2. For a brief introduction of this system of thought, see Brown, *ibid.*, pp. 168 ff.; Macquarrie, *op. cit.*, pp. 301 ff.

shorne (1897–). And if there is one central teacher from which the school can be said to draw its major arguments, it would be the noted mathematician and philosopher, Alfred North Whitehead (1861–1947).

As with many other such radical theologies, process theology also seems to be strongly linked to some particular presuppositions. In this case, it is Whitehead's process philosophy.

The ancient philosophers developed their system around the idea that the world was a fixed thing, that being included becoming. Whitehead developed his system around the idea that the world was dynamic, always changing, that becoming includes being. Even God, according to Whitehead, is subject to becoming. Religion, for him, "is the vision of something which stands beyond, behind and within, the passing flux of immediate things; something which is real and yet waiting to be realized; something which is a remote possibility, and yet the greatest of present facts; something whose possession is the final good and yet is beyond all reach."[3]

Hartshorne developed Whitehead's ideas even further. Whitehead had said that becoming was one of the attributes of God, along with being, infinity, and eternity. Hartshorne said that God is also finite and temporal.[4] Tillich, as we shall see, regards God as being itself. Hartshorne said that God is process itself.[5] The ultimate category is becoming, not being.

Process theology took these developments of Hartshorne and began to apply them more specifically in the theological world. Associated with such English-speaking radical theologians as Norman Pittenger, Daniel Day Williams, Schubert

3. Alfred North Whitehead, *Science and the Modern World* (London: Cambridge University Press, 1936), p. 275.

4. Eric Rust, *Evolutionary Philosophies and Contemporary Theology* (Philadelphia: The Westminster Press, 1969), pp. 177 ff.

5. Daniel Day Williams, *The Spirit and the Forms of Love* (New York: Harper and Row, 1968), pp. 106-109.

Ogden, and John Cobb, Jr., the group "is convinced that, to answer the God-is-dead Theology, we must demonstrate the objective reality of God by a rational metaphysics. Whitehead seems to them a good beginning."[6] There are even those who wonder if Teilhard de Chardin does not belong within this circle.[7] He certainly shared many similar emphases with them.

Though we can be grateful that this new emphasis is seeking to re-assert the metaphysical reality of God in the twentieth century world, we cannot forget that they are seeking to do it by appealing to experience and logical coherence rather than to miraculous, divine disclosure as the sources of truth about God. And it is precisely because of their stand against special revelation that their results finally must be judged as concessive reactions, rather than biblical affirmations.

1. Like Teilhard, process theologians use a starting point which necessarily must be their finish—the self-destructive synthesis of modern man's presuppositions—nature in its autonomy and independence, and man's freedom to subject that world to his own categories. In this case, those human categories are theological. But they are molded by a Kantian prejudice against metaphysics that reduces even theological categories to categories manageable by autonomous man, and not divine givens. In this spirit, process theologians reject the biblical idea of God as being over and above the universe. Instead, to them, all things occur "within God." As one writer has put it, "God is not so

---

6. Hordern, *op. cit.*, p. 248.
7. Eulalio Baltazar, *God Within Process* (New York: Newman Press, 1970), pp. 1-26. Colin Brown, *op. cit.*, p. 241, tries to dissociate Teilhard from the school. To be sure, Teilhard works from the nature-grace schema, but the similarities far outweigh, in my mind, the differences. Brown's analysis here, as in other areas of his study, does not seem to me to take full recognition of the overall presuppositions and structure of Teilhard's thought. Because of this, his critique here may be somewhat shortsighted.

much a being as the dynamic behind evolution, emerging all the time in everything in history and nature."[8] From this basic concept of emerging comes the very name for their emphasis—"process" theology.

Perhaps for this very reason, we have not yet seen much interest in process theology in the "third world." Science—and its omnipresence, its omnipotence—has not yet reached the shaping influence it plays in Western culture and in Japan. The time has not yet fully come for theology's radical need "to come to terms" with science as in the West. The pressure has not yet built enough to create a new third world synthesis theology along the lines of the process theology.

2. Like Teilhard, process theologians compromise the sovereignty of God. God, says Whitehead, is "co-creator of the universe."[9] God's creation is said to be a continuing evolutionary process, a co-existence of order and freedom in which man takes part in determining the future. For this reason, Williams' systematic exposition of process theology contains no section on eschatology. How can it? There is no sovereign God, ordering, molding history and men, at the center of his system.

3. Like Tillich, process theology tends to dissipate the idea of God as a personal being. God is reduced to a principal aspect of the whole of things. Though God is conceded to be "an actual entity," and Hartshorne is even willing to define God as "living person," he immediately tells us that "we doubt if anyone can really mean by a 'person' more than what Whitehead means by a 'personally ordered' sequence of experiences within certain defining characteristics."[10] The personal God of the Bible reveals himself, speaks and acts for himself, declares His purposes intelli-

---

8. C. Brown, *loc. cit.*
9. Rust, *op. cit.*, pp. 108-117.
10. C. Hartshorne and W. L. Reese, eds., *Philosophers Speak of God* (Chicago: University of Chicago Press, 1953), p. 274.

gently. The God of process theology is "a personally ordered sequence of experiences, . . ." a mental concept postulated on the basis of analogies from human experience.

4. Though process theology seeks to give its theory of God biblical overtones, it is a veneer, and not a foundation to the system. As Carl Henry has written, "nonetheless creation becomes evolution, redemption becomes relationship, and resurrection becomes renewal. The supernatural is abandoned, miracles vanish, and the living God of the Bible is submerged in immanental motifs."[11] Against this background, Christ is seen merely as a symbol of divine activity in the world rather than as an "intervention" (to use its word). He is said to be a man in whom God worked rather than God incarnate. The doctrine of the physical resurrection of Christ cannot be held because, says one process theologian, this would have constituted "divine compulsion. . . . Neither human free will nor the normal processes of nature are subjected to, or interrupted by, divine compulsion."[12]

5. Process theology negates its alleged affirmation of God's transcendence by repudiating His supernaturalness and absolute transcendence. God becomes merely an aspect of all reality. As Hartshorne puts it, "God literally contains the universe."[13] Though many of the leaders reject any pantheistic identification of God with the world, the world becomes necessary to God, the world always conditions God's activity. To express this idea, they have coined a new word, "panentheism"—all things occur "within God."

6. Process theology subverts the love of God into a

---

11. Carl F. H. Henry, "The Reality and Identity of God—II," *Christianity Today* XIII, 13 (March 28, 1969), 581.
12. Peter Hamilton, *The Living God and the Modern World* (London: Hodder and Stoughton, 1967), p. 226.
13. Charles Hartshorne, *The Divine Relativity* (New Haven: Yale University Press, 1964), p. 90.

universal principle which extends through Jesus as the Elect man to all mankind (a popular neo-orthodox theme). Williams, professor at Union Seminary, New York, has emphasized this feature particularly in his dismissal of the biblical doctrine of God's electing love. He has also suggested that the doctrine of universal salvation be re-opened for study.[14] In a similar connection, Pittenger considers man permanently valuable to God, perhaps even indispensable.[15] One is tempted to ask, with Carl Henry, how God managed so well before man was created.

---

14. Daniel D. Williams, *op. cit.*, pp. 34-37.
15. Norman Pittenger, *Process Thought and Christian Faith* (New York: Macmillan, 1968), p. 81.

CHAPTER XIII

THEOLOGY OF BEING

There are three theological giants in the twentieth century world. We have studied two of them—Barth and Bultmann—in this work. The third is Paul Tillich (1886–1965). Often called "the theologian's theologian," Tillich shares many things in common with Barth and Bultmann. Like them, Tillich is deeply indebted to existentialism for the philosophical beginnings of his system.[1] Like them, he accepted wholeheartedly the liberal higher criticism of the Bible. Like them, his writing has drawn the attention of philosophers as well as theologians.

But, in spite of the similarities, Tillich has developed "a theological system that defies attempts to put it into any category."[2] And, perhaps partly for this reason, he has founded no distinct theological school. We cannot speak of Tillichism as we speak of Bultmann's form criticism or Barthianism. Nevertheless, though without a school, probably only Rudolf Bultmann has exerted a comparable influence on present-day theology. His influence in Japan, for example, has been rather widespread since the end of World War II.[3] And, though support for his positions in Korea is still rather isolated, it is by no means slight.[4] In 1969–

---

1. Van Til, *The Reformed Pastor and Modern Thought, op. cit.,* pp. 154 ff.
2. Hordern, *op. cit.,* p. 171.
3. Yoshio Noro, *op. cit.,* pp. 67-74.
4. Kan Ha-bae, *op. cit.,* p. 37.

1970 alone, three of Tillich's works appeared in Korean translation.

Part of the reason for Tillich's popularity in academic circles is his passionate concern for relating the biblical message to his contemporary situation. Related to what he calls "the principle of correlation," Tillich's argument is that there must be a correlation between the thought and problems of man and the answers given by religious faith. On the one hand, he continues, naturalistic philosophy cannot answer man's deepest questions because it finds answers in man's own natural existence. On the other hand, he also repudiates the answer of what we would call historic Christian supernaturalism because, according to him, it sees the Christian message as "a set of sacred truths that have fallen into the human situation like strange bodies from a strange world."[5] How, then, shall we find our answers?

1. According to Tillich, we begin by redefining religion. Religion is not a matter of certain beliefs or practices. A man is religious at the point where he is "ultimately concerned."[6] An ultimate concern is one that takes precedence over all of the other concerns of life. The ultimate concern grasps a man and lifts him out of himself. It is the total commitment of oneself, one's world.

2. What ought to concern us ultimately? "Our ultimate concern is that which determines our being or non-being." We become ultimately concerned with that which we believe to have the power of destroying or saving our very being, the whole of human reality, the structure, the meaning and the aim of existence. The ultimate is Being itself, or what we traditionally have called God.[7]

3. God, to Tillich, is neither a thing nor a being. God is beyond being and beyond things. God is Being itself,

---

5. Hordern, *op. cit.*, p. 173.
6. Paul Tillich, *Systematic Theology* (London: Nesbet and Co., Ltd., 1955), I, p. 15.
7. *Ibid.*, pp. 261 ff.

the power of being, the ground of being. Even to regard God as the highest being would reduce him to the level of a creature. In the same way, it is just as atheistic, according to Tillich, to affirm the existence of God as to deny it. For, he continues, Being itself transcends existence. God is man's symbolic answer to the search for courage that overcomes the anxiety of man's boundary situation between being and non-being. A more popular rendering of this same point of view can be found in Bishop John Robinson's *Honest to God.*

4. In this same light, Tillich redefines sin in terms of being and estrangement from being.[8] According to Tillich, it is not some classic concept of sin which is responsible for the tensions of modern life. It is estrangement from the ground of our being.

5. Christ, according to Tillich, is the symbol in whom estrangement is overcome, a symbol of the "New Being" in which every force of estrangement trying to dissolve his unity with God has been dissolved. The importance of the word "symbol" cannot be overemphasized. Tillich rejects radically all orthodox interpretations of the person and work of Christ. According to Tillich, for example, the assertion that "God has become man" is "not a paradoxical but a nonsensical statement."[9] The biblical accounts of the crucifixion are "often contradictory legendary reports."[10] While he admits that the resurrection is more than "the manifestation of a bodiless spirit," he says that to ask about the molecules of the physical body of Jesus is to compound absurdity with blasphemy. For Tillich, the resurrection story simply means that Jesus is "restored to the dignity of the Christ in the mind of the disciples."[11]

---

8. *Ibid.*, p. 263.
9. Paul Tillich, *Systematic Theology* (Chicago: University of Chicago Press, 1957), II, p. 109.
10. *Ibid.*, p. 178.
11. *Ibid.*, p. 182.

6. How does man share in this conquest of estrangement from being? The traditional answers of regeneration, justification, and sanctification are reinterpreted. Regeneration becomes "the state of having been drawn into the new reality manifest in Jesus" as the bearer of the New Being.[12] Justification is no sovereign act of a personal God. It is a symbol-word to designate that man is accepted in spite of himself.[13] Sanctification also is redefined as the process by which the power of New Being transforms personality and community both inside and outside the church. In this way, the New Being manifested in Christ is said to answer man's ultimate concern and his quest for the ground of all being. Man is found by the power beyond him that heals his existential conflicts and overcomes his estrangement from himself, from others, from his ground of being.

The most charitable judgment of Tillich's work is to recognize it as "an impressive accomplishment, the product of a supple, precise, encyclopedic, and immensely creative mind. But it is not so much Christian theology as a translation of Christian theology into the language of theosophical-ontological speculation. Sometimes, the translation helps us to see the original in a clearer light. But, more often, the translation does violence to both the spirit and the letter of that which it translates."[14]

1. Basic to Tillich's failure is his rejection of the Bible as the revealed Word of God applicable to this age. For it, Tillich has substituted philosophy in his effort to analyze contemporary man's deepest problems of existence. Tillich's fundamental fault is not that he has substituted philosophy for theology, as the critic Kenneth Hamilton has charged.[15] His fault is that he has substituted man's word for God's

---

12. *Ibid.*, p. 204.
13. *Ibid.*, p. 206.
14. Kenneth Hamilton, "Paul Tillich," *Creative Minds in Contemporary Theology, op. cit.*, p. 479.
15. *Ibid.*, pp. 469-471.

Word. As Colin Brown has rightly said, "for theology, the primary datum is God's revelation of Himself in Christ, as witnessed to by Scripture . . . (Matt. 5:17 ff.; Luke 24:27; John 5:39-47; I Cor. 1:15-31). While theological truth illuminates life in general, it can only be discovered from the Word of God. Tillich, however, reverses the process and makes his version of general truth the test of revelation."[16]

2. Tillich's "principle of correlation" argues that philosophy can give us a proper analysis of the human situation but only the "saved" reason can be expected to see the answer to the situation clearly. Tillich assumes far too much neutrality for man's reason. How can a philosophical reason not touched by the Christian faith correctly formulate the structures and meaning of human existence? Paul reminds us that reason without Christ is a dirty window that needs washing. And dirty windows, in opposition to Tillich's theories, do not let light in.[17]

3. Tillich's doctrine of God has no relation to the biblical doctrine. It is certainly difficult to see with what propriety Tillich uses the word "God" in any Christian sense. As another has said, "It is hardly Trinitarian. His idea is not personal in any familiar or traditional sense. It is more an all-pervading, rational power but not a person who communicates and with whom man can enter into communion. Tillich's view of being more often seems to be an aspect of this world rather than a God who exists over and above it and who is independent of it."[18] The biblical distinction of Creator and creature has vanished in Tillich's system. What kind of a God is the God beyond theism? What kind of a God is the God who is neither supernatural nor natural? "Tillich apparently does not want to choose between the alternatives in front of him. A geometrician may have a concept of the square and he may

16. C. Brown, *op. cit.*, pp. 199-200.
17. Van Til, *op. cit.*, pp. 162-167.
18. C. Brown, *op. cit.*, p. 199.

have a concept of the circle. But he cannot have a square circle."[19]

4. Tillich's Christology reduces Jesus to a symbol.[20] Of himself, Jesus is nothing. The significant thing is simply that "He remained transparent to the divine mystery until His death, which was the final manifestation of His transparency."[21] We are left with what has been criticized as "a diluted Christology which might be acceptable to a Hindu or a Buddhist. They can accept everything in Tillich's exposition, except precisely the fact that Jesus Himself and no other was, and is, and ever shall be, the Christ."[22]

5. Tillich's soteriology has no concrete meaning except as another symbol to describe an existential situation which has no relation to the living God. What it basically amounts to is an awakening in man to a new self through "meditating" upon the death and resurrection "symbols" of Christ. Those uncommitted to the Christian faith can find equal saving power by applying Tillich's methodology to the contemplation of Buddha or Confucius. Tillich keeps the shell, and throws away the kernel.

---

19. Cf. Robert L. Reymond, *Introductory Studies in Contemporary Theology* (Nutley, N. J.: Presbyterian and Reformed Publishing Co., 1968), pp. 199-237.

20. David H. Freeman, *Tillich* (Philadelphia: Presbyterian and Reformed Publishing Co., 1962), pp. 39 ff.

21. Tillich, *op. cit.*, I, 149 ff.

22. G. H. Tavard, *Paul Tillich and the Christian Message* (London: Burns and Oates, 1962), p. 167.

CHAPTER XIV

MYSTICISM

It is not a long step to move from much of modern-day thinking to mysticism, from Tillich's "theology of being" to the slogans of Zen Buddhism. Both are guilty of a common error—the obliteration of a clear line between the Creator and the creature. In this connection, the recent admission of a Zen Buddhist who spoke of his admiration of Barth because their views were so similar underlines this connecting link.[1] It appears that there are greater similarities in terms of more basic agreement between Barthianism and Shamanism, for example, than many are willing to concede. There may have been no halo forming around the head of Karl Barth when he preached, as there is said to have been around the head of Elder Park Tae-sun, leader of the Olive-tree sect in Korea. But both Barth and Elder Park move in a circle which may look more or less concentric, but whose center is more subjectivism than God.

Mysticism is not some movement special to the Near or the Far East, or even to Asia's more extreme sects. It may be found around the world, and its elements or characteristics may sometimes be found in places where its more systematic form would be unwelcome. Frank Gaynor has defined its essence as "any philosophy, doctrine, teaching

---

1. Gempo Hoshino, *Antwort;* Karl Barth zum siebzigsten Geburtstag am 10. Mai, 1956 (Zolliken-Zurich, 1956), p. 423, as quoted by Cornelius Van Til, *The Confession of 1967* (Philadelphia: Presbyterian and Reformed Publishing Co., 1967), p. 125.

or belief centered more on the worlds of the Spirit than the material universe, and aimed at the spiritual union or mental oneness with the Universal Spirit, through inductive and emotional apprehension of spiritual reality, and through various forms of spiritual contemplation or disciplines. Mysticism in its simplest and most essential meaning is a type of religion which puts the emphasis on immediate awareness of relation with God, direct and intimate consciousness of Divine Presence."[2] It is particularly the strong element of subjectivity and directness of revelation that forms the common link between neo-orthodoxy and Timothy Leary's new "religion of inner space." We may understand it better if we look for elements, rather than movements.

1. Its central feature will be belief in special revelation outside the Bible.[3] The mystic may say that the Bible is merely a witness to revelation, waiting for God's presence in dialogue with the sinner to become special revelation. This is the position of Barth and his worldwide disciples. Or he may say that God still speaks to us directly in dreams and visions. God is then said to add, not new revelations, but new interpretations to the Bible. Joseph Smith, the founder of the Mormon Church, believed that God had given him a new interpretation of the Bible.[4] Ellen G. White, the prophetess-spokesman of the Seventh-day Adventist Church, is still regarded as a prophet of the Lord, like Moses, gifted with special revelation.[5] One often finds a similar emphasis in the literature of what has come to be called Neo-Pentecostalism. God is said to grant, not only the gift of tongues, but also special revelation apart from

2. Frank Gaynor, *Dictionary of Mysticism* (New York: Philosophical Library, 1953), p. 119.
3. Edwin Palmer, *The Holy Spirit* (Philadelphia: Presbyterian and Reformed Publishing Co., 1958), pp. 101 ff.
4. Anthony A. Hoekema, *The Four Major Cults* (Grand Rapids: Eerdmans Publishing Co., 1963), pp. 9 ff.
5. *Ibid.*, pp. 96-98.

the Bible.[6] In this same light, many Asian evangelicals, seeking an answer for a very difficult problem in their life, go to a nearby mountain for prayer and fasting, and return after forty days, saying that God has appeared to them in a vision and given them the answer to their problem. These people all share one thing in common—the mystical belief that God speaks apart from His Word, the Bible.

2. With the loss of an objective standard, mysticism emphasizes subjectivism and emotionalism. In the sixteenth century Reformation in Europe, in the movement called Anabaptism, this feature appeared among certain groups who remembered the example of Isaiah and walked naked through the streets.[7] In America, it appeared in groups like the "Quakers," whose nickname indicated their habit of quaking when they felt "the presence of God," or in the "Holy Rollers," who would roll on the floors when God's revelation came.[8] In Korea, it appears in clapping hands, and screaming and tears during the worship services of the Olive-tree sect, centered around Elder Park, the self-designated "Holy Spirit." In far less violent fashion, but equally subjective, it manifests itself in the remarks of Paul Tillich on the question of the reliability of the record concerning Jesus' miracles. "In history, of course, you never have definite evidence for anything," he had replied to a reporter. The reporter's perceptiveness caught fully the thrust of that remark. "But how, I insisted, could symbols change, even lose all meaning, without affecting the content of the Christian message? . . . This was such a thorough-going kind of relativism."[9]

3. Mysticism usually deemphasizes the established church

---

6. John R. W. Stott, *The Baptism and Fullness of the Holy Spirit* (Chicago: Inter-Varsity Fellowship, 1964), is a helpful exegetical discussion of the question of tongues.

7. R. A. Knox, *Enthusiasm* (Oxford: Oxford University Press, 1950), pp. 135-138.

8. *Ibid.*, pp. 139 ff.

9. Ved Mehta, *op. cit.*, p. 49.

and is one-leader-centered. There is often a strong attack on the uselessness and corruption of the church. The 144,000 of Revelation chapter 7 may be limited to Jehovah's Witnesses or, as in the Adventist Church, to those who worship on Saturday and not Sunday, who do not have "the mark of the beast."[10] Or, as in the theology of secularization, the effort will be to break down the lines between church and world, and underline the inabilities of the church, as presently constituted, to speak to the world's needs. Often with this emphasis, there will be the promotion of a movement whose center may be one person in particular—Ellen White of the Seventh-day Adventist Church, Joseph Smith of the Mormon Church, Elder Park of the Korean Olive-tree sect, Dietrich Bonhoeffer, the prophet of "religionless Christianity."

4. Mystical emphasis is placed on the spectacular. It is not the ordinary gifts of the Spirit, but the extraordinary gifts of the Spirit, that are emphasized. The revivalists call out, "Grace! Visions! Miracles! Tongues!" Miracles are stressed and sometimes also the so-called gift of tongues. Behind the history of many of Africa's new "Christo-syncristic religions [*sic*]," one finds healers are miracle-workers.[11]

5. Mysticism emphasizes eschatology in some limiting sense. To those mystics on a scale sliding closer to a recognition of biblical authority, it will be eschatology severely limited to the events of the second coming of Christ, often involving itself in the closest investigation of details surrounding this event, often emphasizing judgment primarily, and not salvation. In sixteenth century Europe, this tendency expressed itself in those extreme elements of Anabaptism who anticipated momentarily the second coming of Christ—the imminent, visible return of Christ to Europe

---

10. Herbert S. Bird, *Theology of Seventh-Day Adventism* (Grand Rapids: Eerdmans Publishing Co., 1961), pp. 93 ff.

11. G. C. Oosthuizen, *Post-Christianity in Africa* (Grand Rapids: Eerdmans Publishing Co., 1968), pp. 119 ff.

to set up His millennial reign. In twentieth century Korea, the same tendency appears in the writings of men like the Rev. Lee Rye-ja, who warns us that the day of grace has passed and that the day of blood and vengeance has come. You can see it in the Korean bookstores, where there are countless collections of sermons on eschatology and more commentaries on the book of Revelation than any other Bible book.

For those mystics further away from the restrictions of biblical authority, eschatology is usually denuded of any references to the second coming of Christ. For Moltmann, it is orientation toward the future, not the coming Christ. For Bultmann, it is demythologized into the existential horizon of human life, that which confronts man with the ultimate meaning of his existence, that which calls him to existential decision. For Barth, "the men of the New Testament were not joyful because they expected that Christ was soon to return on the clouds of heaven. On the contrary, they looked for Christ's second coming because the presence of Christ with them was already so gloriously real."[12]

Mysticism at least reminds us that our Christianity must be more than merely talking Christianity. It must be Christianity of the heart and of the emotions. At the same time, "beloved, do not believe every spirit, but test the spirits, to see whether they are of God" (I John 4:11). A test of mysticism's spirit should note the following dangers at least.

1. Mysticism's emphasis on special revelation apart from the Bible forgets that "the word of God is the only rule to direct us how we may glorify and enjoy him."[13] We may know only that will of God for our life which is necessary to know (Deut. 18:18). But that will of God we can find only in the Bible.[14] If we seek for "teaching, for reproof,

---

12. Hordern, *op. cit.*, p. 144.
13. *Westminster Shorter Catechism*, Q. 2.
14. Oliver Barclay, *Guidance* (Chicago: Inter-Varsity Fellowship, 1956).

for correction, for instruction in righteousness" (II Tim. 3:16-17), there is only one place to which we can turn— the Bible. The evangelical who resorts to dreams and visions is as guilty of mysticism's basic fault as Barth, who also divides the Bible from the revelation of God. Both forget that God's Word has been written.

2. Mysticism tends to forget that a balance is needed regarding the use of the emotions. We are not to deny our emotions. We must still "love the Lord . . . with all your heart and with all your soul and with all your mind" (Luke 22:37). Mysticism tends to let emotions control our faith. On the contrary, our faith must control our emotions.

3. Mysticism's attacks on the church and its tendency to replace the church with the leadership of one man distort the biblical picture of the church and its ministers. Paul could speak with great firmness concerning the corruption and inabilities of the church (I Cor. 1:10 ff.; 6:15 ff.; 11: 20-21; 15:12) but he could also see the "grace of God which is given you by Jesus Christ" (I Cor. 1:4), and he could therefore call "them that are sanctified in Christ Jesus, called to be saints" as existing in fellowship "with all that in every place call upon the name of Jesus Christ our Lord," and "the church of God which is at Corinth" (I Cor. 1:2). Paul could not limit the membership and vitality of the church beyond those limits set by God himself.

So also, Paul offers no distorted picture of some super-role for the minister. To the church at Corinth, which expressed such tendencies, Paul asks, not, "Who is Apollos? Who is Paul . . . ," but rather, "What then is Apollos? What is Paul?" (I Cor. 3:5). Paul looked on himself, not as a man, but as a tool which God used, "servants through whom you believed, as the Lord assigned to each." The church which has an over-exaggerated view of the importance of its ministers moves dangerously toward mysticism.

4. Mysticism's tendency to stress the spectacular gifts

of the Spirit often leads it into a neglect of the more abiding value of the ordinary gifts (I Cor. 12:31; 13:1, 8). It often suggests that such unusual spiritual experiences as the so-called "gift of tongues" are the secret of holiness and usefulness. Many in the history of the church have been powerful in character and ministry without them, while the Corinthians, who had some of them, remained carnal. Even if such special gifts of the Spirit are thought to be present,[15] they must be exercised, as all gifts of the Spirit, within the limitations set by God in His Word (I Cor. 14). "For God is not a God of confusion but of peace" (I Cor. 14:33).

5. Mysticism's emphasis on certain features of biblical eschatology distorts the balance of Scripture. The center of biblical eschatology is neither judgment on sinners nor salvation for God's people nor any program which restricts biblical perspectives to present-day concerns, a la Moltmann or Bultmann. The center of eschatology is the coming of God in Christ with power and glory. Even our emphasis on the millennium cannot replace our emphasis on the great fact of eschatology—the final manifestation of the glory of God in Christ. Unfortunately, sometimes even conservatives fail in reminding us again and again of that overarching center. And again, eschatology in this light means much more than simply the second coming of Christ. It includes also the first coming of Christ (Heb. 1:1-2; Acts 2:17; I John 2:18). But again this must be seen as that preliminary display of glory which shall find fulfillment in the new Jerusalem.

---

15. John H. Skilton, "Special Gifts for a Special Age," *Presbyterian Guardian* XL, 10 (Dec., 1971), 145-147, presents a strong case for the classic Reformed position, i.e., that such gifts have now ceased.

CHAPTER XV

PIETISM

The writing of this chapter in our study brings us to "a great gulf fixed" between everything that has preceded us and everything that follows us. It is a gulf that basically divides all systems of thought on one side and all systems of thought on the other. The gulf is the trustworthiness of Scripture. Those who confess the inerrancy and authority of the Bible stand on one side of the gulf. Those who do not stand on the other.

In this sense, though we have seen the diversity of viewpoint between Cullmann's "salvation history" school and Tillich's "theology of being," we can see also the unifying principle that enables us to regard them as members of the same family, but living in different cities. Their systems, to a greater or lesser degree, do not ultimately seek to do full justice to the Bible as the Word of God. In this sense also, the remaining theological movements we shall be treating, though just as diverse, are all just as single in their desire to subject themselves to the complete integrity of the Bible. They are united in their zeal to listen to the Lord, speaking in His Word. And so our criticism is tempered by the bond that remains a symbol of our family unity—full obedience to the Word of the Father.

This does not mean we are, thereby, automatically freed from self-criticism. For in the struggle between historical Protestantism and what Van Til and others have called "post-Kantian thought," we have not always challenged the would-be autonomous man in terms of the self-interpreting Christ of the Scriptures. "It is the Christ of Scripture and the false Christ of would-be-autonomous man that must be seen as engaged in mortal combat. Reformed Christians will find themselves responsible for taking the leadership in this challenge. For it is only in the Reformed Faith that the self-interpreting Christ of Scripture is accepted without compromise."[1] In the evangelical circles operating outside of Calvinism, "concessions are made to the very principles of continuity and discontinuity derived from apostate thought. In their doctrine of the will of man as free so far as it is independent of God, these forms of Christianity have, in a measure, yielded to the idea of metaphysical and ethical or ultimate freedom found in all apostate thought, but expressed more clearly in Kant and in post-Kantian theology, philosophy, and science."[2]

One of the deepest influences on historic Christianity appeared in 1675 when a Lutheran pastor in Germany, Philip Spener (1635–1705) published a little book, called in Latin, *Heartfelt Desire*.[3] The appearance of the book marked the birth of pietism.

Spener was disturbed by the coldness and aridity of the Protestant church. Contemporary preaching was sterile. The sermon had become "an artificial rhetorical speech pieced together from the Bible." So a seventeenth century sermon on Matthew 10:30 ("But the very hairs of your head are all numbered") could be constructed by outlining (1) the origin, style, form, and natural position of our hair, (2) the correct care of the hair, (3) reminiscences, reminders, warnings, and comfort derived from the hair, (4) how to care for the hair in a good Christian fashion and to make use of it.

---

1. Van Til, *The Great Debate Today, op. cit.*, p. 22.
2. *Loc. cit.*
3. Philip Spener, *Pia Desideria* (Philadelphia: Fortress Press, 1964).

Against the background of preaching and thinking like this, pietism arose as a protest of living faith against a lifeless and impersonal religion. Through Spener's book, an analysis of contemporary weaknesses was made—corrupt practices, worldly clergy, formalism, lack of mission. Five proposals were made to correct these abuses: (1) A more extensive use of the Word of God, (2) A diligent exercise of spiritual priesthood, (3) The preaching of faith, (4) A loving spirit in controversy, (5) The devotional nurture and pastoral training of theological students.[4]

To implement these demands, Spener and fellow colleagues like Francke (1663–1727) gathered the serious minded into small groups for Bible study and mutual assistance in spiritual growth. He called these gatherings "little churches inside the church." He established centers of fellowship, the *collegia pietatis* as the groups were called. But the central purpose of these associations of piety was not scholarship but evangelism, the dissemination of the Word of God through all classes of society. Along with this program went a strong self-discipline which included abstinence from playing cards, dancing and the theatre, and moderation in food, drink, and dress.

The movement did not leave untouched also the area of compassion. Since Christianity was the practice of a transforming way of life, good works became the outward expression of that faith. Faith was the sun, good works were the sun's rays. Schools, orphanages, and other philanthropic organizations were started. The work of foreign missions was a unique feature of the pietist movement.[5]

As the years passed, pietism's influence touched many nations. In the eighteenth century, the life of John Wesley was molded and rekindled by the fire of pietism. And, through Wesley's preaching and the movement that led to

---

4. *Ibid.*, pp. 87 ff.
5. John T. McNeill, *Modern Christian Movements* (New York: Harper Torchbooks, 1968), pp. 49 ff.

the formation of the Methodist Church, revival came to England. In America, pietism joined forces with Calvinists like Jonathan Edwards to bring revival to the new nation. In the nineteenth and twentieth centuries, the preaching of Dwight L. Moody bore strong traces of pietism's emphases. Once again a fresh interest in the old earmarks of the movement was kindled—devotional preaching; the uselessness of doctrine when unrelated to life; abstinence from certain habits, such as smoking, drinking, theatre attendance, in promotion of the distinctive traits of what came to be called the "separated life"; new passion for foreign missions; the establishment of schools where the devotional life could be emphasized.[6] All these emphases remain as an integral part of American "conservative" theology today.

But pietism did not stop in America. For during this general period, the evangelical, fired by his faith, "freely overleaped national boundaries" and carried to the ends of the world his new-found word of hope. For the first time, in many Eastern lands, the gospel was brought by missionaries, many of them deeply touched by pietistic emphases. Now pietism, through the missionary, left its stamp on the life of the church in many areas. In Korea, for example, it helped to produce a lack of doctrinal preaching and an emphasis on devotional preaching, the cultivation of the Christian life sometimes largely in terms of the practice of, or abstinence from, certain practices; a healthy emphasis on the devotional life and personal evangelism; an early church whose center was the layman and not the minister; a stress on emotions rather than intellect, revival rather than reformation, introspection rather than service.

The positive contribution of pietism is enormous, and the good far outweighs the bad. It kindled a healthy concern for true piety, in the face of almost no piety at all. It improved pastoral training. It breathed spiritual life into what

6. *Ibid.*, pp. 91 ff.

might otherwise have been a dead or sterile substitute for orthodoxy. It initiated perhaps the greatest missionary and evangelistic program Christianity has ever known. It led to far-reaching and powerful action for the poor and oppressed of many lands. It inspired some of the church's greatest hymns (Charles Wesley) and contributed to some of the world's greatest music (Handel and Bach).

At the same time, it has weaknesses which have continued to plague the Western, and now the Eastern, church.

1. Its stress on experience could easily degenerate into subjectivism and even mysticism.[7] Its emphasis on introspection sometimes degenerated into a morbid preoccupation with the state of the individual soul. This element forms an especially remarkable parallel with the similar feature of mysticism, which we indicated in an earlier chapter. The results of this might be seen in the system of liberalism developed by Schleiermacher (1768–1834), whose epistemological center was religion as "feeling." Schleiermacher had been trained in a pietist home and a Moravian college.

2. Emotion was so strongly emphasized in pietism that the role of the intellect was seriously harmed. Pietism failed to keep spiritual vitality and intellectual vigor in proper balance. As a result, pietism, as a theological force, remained then and now relatively sterile. It remains suspicious of science, philosophy, and the academic world.

3. It cannot see the wider demands of the Christian faith in areas like politics, society, or labor. Christianity is said by the pietist to participate in society only insofar as it calls the sinner to repentance and faith in Christ. It does not demand a Christian approach to education or science or economics. It demands only that an individual Christian approach education or science or economics.

4. Pietism frequently underemphasized doctrine and overemphasized the practical frequently. This lack of doc-

---

7. Ronald Knox, *op. cit.*, pp. 535 ff.

played some part in the development of the ecumenical movement mirrored in the World Council of Churches. And it continues to be evident in that movement's doctrinal latitudinarianism. It also continues to leave pietistically influenced movements more open to theological deviations and perversions. For this reason, and in view of the strong influence of pietism on the so-called "mission fields," there is much room for concern that the "younger" churches will be easily prone to unbiblical movements and elements. A quick glance at Oosthuizen's *Post Christianity In Africa* confirms this.

(5.) Pietism historically has tended also to produce the "little church within the church," with a real danger of what some have called disruption and spiritual pride. In the nineteenth century, this tendency helped to create inter-denominational, independent foreign mission agencies, such as the justly famous China Inland Mission (now the Over-seas Missionary Fellowship). Such groups, rather skeptical of the holiness of the established churches, have maintained separate existence to the present day, and continue to mani-fest many of the pietistic emphases we have cited earlier.

(6.) Pietism tends to allow devotional routines of Bible reading, prayer, and church attendance to become a sub-stitute for fuller Christian practice. Its tendency to limit the definition of the Christian life to the four walls of a church building or the abstinence from certain practices produces an abstracted view of "spiritual life." The wider responsi-bilities of love and peace and longsuffering can sometimes take second place to a stronger emphasis on prohibitions regarding smoke or drink. "These ought ye to have done and not to leave the other undone . . ." (Matt. 23:23).

105

CHAPTER XVI

DISPENSATIONALISM

In the nineteenth century in England and Ireland, a new movement of biblical interpretation arose within the conservative orbit. Deeply concerned about what they felt to be the dead hand of tradition and legalism in the Church of England, one man in particular, John Nelson Darby (1800–1882) began to gather together dissatisfied Christians for weekly Bible study and weekly observance of the Lord's Supper. The group began to be called "the brethren" or "the Plymouth brethren" (Plymouth, England, was one of the strongest of the early centers of the movement). Resembling to a great extent the organizational structure of the Non-church movement in Japan, the brethren admitted any professing Christian to their informal services, refused to acknowledge or create any special system of clergy, conducted their meetings without order of service, and insisted that this was a return to the New Testament pattern of church government and worship.[1]

A new approach to the interpretation of biblical prophecy now began to emerge from their meetings. Called popularly "dispensationalism," it quickly gained acceptance in evangelical circles. The founder, Darby, made seven speaking tours to the United States, and by the end of the nineteenth century, American fundamentalism had been deeply affected

1. Clarence Bass, *Backgrounds to Dispensationalism* (Grand Rapids: Eerdmans Publishing Co., 1960), pp. 48 ff.

106

by the theology of the brethren movement.[2] Prophetic Bible conferences were organized on a nationwide basis and these became largely dominated by dispensational emphases. The Bible Study Conferences associated with the name of Dwight L. Moody were virtually controlled by dispensationalists.[3] The school founded by Moody, later called the Moody Bible Institute, became a center for the teaching. In 1909, a special study edition of the King James Version of the Bible was printed, the so-called Scofield Reference Edition of the Bible. The notes it contained were dispensational in emphasis, and the Bible became a great aid in solidifying and popularizing the system.[4]

Since the influence of dispensationalism was particularly strong among conservative-minded Presbyterians, it is not surprising to find dispensationalism a very strong part of the Presbyterian Church, and particularly so in the lands of the "younger churches."[5]

Though it is often confused with historic premillennialism, the majority of its distinctive doctrines are not held by historic premillennialism. All dispensationalists are premillenarians, but not all premillenarians are dispensationalists.

1. Dispensationalists (unlike historic premillenarians) insist always on an exactly literal interpretation of Scripture. They denounce as "spiritualizers" or "allegorizers" those who do not interpret the Bible with the same degree of literalness as they do. In this connection, they insist on an unconditional literal fulfillment of all prophetic promises.[6] So, on this interpretation, the Old Testament promises to

---

2. C. Norman Kraus, *Dispensationalism in America* (Richmond: John Knox Press, 1958), pp. 45 ff.

3. *Ibid.*, pp. 71 ff.

4. Oswald T. Allis, *Prophecy and the Church* (Philadelphia: Presbyterian and Reformed Publishing Co., 1945), pp. 9 ff.

5. For some analysis of its influence in Korea, see Harvie M. Conn, "Studies in the Theology of the Korean Presbyterian Church," *Westminster Theological Journal* XXIX, 1 (Nov., 1966), 50-53.

6. Bass, *op. cit.*, pp. 21-24.

Israel must be said to be earthly promises to an earthly people, to be fulfilled upon this earth. The temple of Ezekiel 40–48 is said to be an earthly temple that will be set up in the millennium. The "new Jerusalem" of Revelation 22 will be the earthly city we know now, the eternal abode of the saints continuing on earth.

2. Since all Old Testament prophecies must be interpreted literally, dispensationalism (unlike historic premillennialism) refuses to admit any relation between the Old Testament Israel and the New Testament church. In fact, it is said that there is not a single prophecy in the Old Testament regarding the church at all. The New Testament church is said to be a mystery parenthesis unknown to the Old Testament prophets. The Old Testament prophecies were made to Israel the earthly nation, and they must be fulfilled literally to Israel, the earthly nation.

3. Dispensationalism (unlike historic premillennialism) says that God's history of dealing with man is the history of seven different dispensations. In each dispensation, God places man under different responsibilities, and in each dispensation God deals with man in a different way.[7] The longest of such dispensations in the Old Testament is said to be the dispensation of law (which is said to extend from the giving of the law on Mount Sinai through most of the public ministry of Christ). We are said to be now in the dispensation of grace. And this will extend to the final dispensation of the kingdom (the millennium).

4. Dispensationalism (unlike historic premillennialism), though it affirms that the sinner is saved in every age by grace, affirms also that law and grace are radically distinct. The effect is to create a multiple basis for God's dealing with man. In the same way, they argue, in the New Testament dispensation of grace, there is no revelation of the law as binding on the New Testament people of God. We, of the

7. C. I. Scofield, *Rightly Dividing the Word of Truth* (Oakland: Western Book and Tract Co., n.d.), p. 18.

dispensation of grace, therefore are under no obligation to obey the ten commandments as a rule of life and faith. Under the dispensation of grace, men are required only to repent and turn in faith to Christ. Under the dispensation of the law, they are required only to obey the law.[8]

(5.) Dispensationalism (unlike historic premillennialism) says that the kingdom Jesus offered to the Jews was not a spiritual kingdom, but the earthly restoration of the Davidic kingdom of the Old Testament.[9] When the Jews rejected their king, Jesus postponed the coming of this earthly kingdom until the millennium. And, as a "great parenthesis," in the meantime, He set up the church. The church, says the dispensationalist, has nothing to do with the kingdom. There is no sense in which we can speak of the kingdom as here now. It is exclusively a future event.[10]

(6.) Dispensationalism (unlike historic premillennialism) says that before the great tribulation of the last days the church will be secretly raptured into the air to meet Jesus. After the rapture a Jewish remnant will take the place of the church as God's instrument on earth for the conversion of Israel and the nations.[11]

Along with all supernaturalists, dispensationalists seek to do full justice to the message of the infallible Bible. They also seek to emphasize, in properly biblical perspective, the second coming of Christ and the consummation of all things. Their zeal for evangelism has, for a long time, been only one of their badges of honor. But their system as a whole seems to this writer to be different from the biblical perspective at several points.

(1.) Their severe emphasis on a literal interpretation of

8. William E. Cox, *An Examination of Dispensationalism* (Philadelphia: Presbyterian and Reformed Publishing Co., 1963), pp. 17-21.

9. Allis, *op. cit.*, pp. 75 ff.

10. Bass, *op. cit.*, pp. 29-33.

11. C. C. Ryrie, *Dispensationalism Today* (Chicago: Moody Press, 1965), pp. 132 ff.

Scripture forgets that Scripture itself often interprets other parts of Scripture in a spiritual, and not literal, way. So, for example, when Amos 9:11-12 speaks of "the restoration of David's booth which has fallen down," James, in Acts 15:15-20, tells us that this prophecy was fulfilled not in the earthly Israel's restoration but in the ingathering of the Gentiles into the church.[12] When God promises David "to establish the throne of his kingdom forever" (II Sam. 7:13), we find the fulfillment of this promise, not in the earthly restoration of David's throne, but in the coming of Christ, "descended from David according to the flesh" (Rom. 1:3; Acts 2:29-32).

2. Dispensationalists forget that, according to the New Testament, the church is "the new Israel" (Rom. 9:6; Gal. 6:16), "a Jew" (Rom. 2:28-29), "the seed of Abraham" (Gal. 3:29), "Zion" (I Peter 2:6; Heb. 12:22). Those who are washed in the blood of Christ have become the new "twelve tribes" (James 1:1), "the strangers scattered" among the nations (I Peter 1:1).

3. Dispensationalism, by its sharp distinction between law and grace, undermines the permanency of grace and the permanency of law. It almost implies that in the Old Testament people were saved by obedience to the law, and it clearly ignores the revelation of God's sovereign grace as early as Adam's need (Gen. 3:15).[13] Its breaking up of the Bible into seven dispensations tends greatly to neglect the unity of God's way of salvation—by grace through faith (Heb. 11:1 ff.).

4. Dispensationalism overemphasizes the idea of the kingdom of God as exclusively future and thereby ignores the fact that the kingdom of God is also present in Christ (Matt. 12:28; Luke 17:21). Instead of seeing the kingdom as Christ-centered (Acts 28:23, 31), they have, with the

---

12. Allis, *op. cit.*, pp. 145-150.
13. Ryrie, *op. cit.*, pp. 184, 186.

early disciples, mistakenly assumed that the kingdom was Israel-centered (Acts 1:6).

(5) The dispensational idea of a "secret" rapture of the church, unknown to non-Christians, seems completely against the thrust of I Thessalonians 4:16-17. There can be no secrets when the Bible speaks of "shouts," "the voice of the archangel," "the trump of God." If the noise awakes the dead, it surely can be no secret.[14]

(6) Amillennialists and premillennialists alike see clearly that the church must pass through the great tribulation (Matt. 24:21-22). As others have indicated, the pretribulation rapture theory of dispensationalism is rooted in the principle of interpretation which separates the church from the total redemptive plan of God.[15] The church must be raptured out of the world before the tribulation because it is not a part of the soon-to-be-restored Davidic kingdom.

---

14. Allis, *op. cit.*, pp. 181 ff.
15. Bass, *op. cit.*, pp. 38-41.

CHAPTER XVII

FUNDAMENTALISM

One of the most vilified words in today's theological vocabulary is "fundamentalism." Even Asia has not escaped this pattern. Emil Brunner, one of the world's leaders of neo-orthodoxy, visited Korea in 1949 and commented that "Korea is open for the gospel but fundamentalism prevents Korea from becoming Christian! And all this because of a man-made, judaistic theory which has nothing to do whatever with the New Testament message of Jesus. . . ."[1]

Since 1949, the language has become stronger. Dr. Harold Hong, the president of the Methodist Seminary, Seoul, says that "extreme fundamentalism" has been the predominant theological trend in the Korean church. "Obscurantism, Puritan ethics, and sectarian perfectionism have been playing a dominant role in the churches."[2] Dr. Kim Chaichoon attacks the theological education of what he calls Korea's "strict fundamentalism," as "a kind of indoctrination of certain fundamental creeds, with no room for objective criticism. . . . The outlook of churchmen tended to become extremely other-worldly, with a strong legalistic and mystical bias."[3] Dr. Rhee Jong-sung, president of the Pres-

1. Quoted in Harvie M. Conn, "Studies in the Theology of the Korean Presbyterian Church—Part I," *Westminster Theological Journal* XXIX, 1 (Nov., 1966), 42-43.

2. Harold S. Hong, "General Picture of the Korean Church, Yesterday and Today," *Korea Struggles for Christ* (Seoul: Christian Literature Society, 1966), pp. 22-23.

3. *Ibid.*, p. 32.

byterian Theological Seminary, Seoul, has called fundamentalism "neo-Pharisaism."[4] Fundamentalism is accused of isolating the church from a knowledge of liberal theology, of extremism, of obscurantism. Are the charges true? What is fundamentalism?

Part of the difficulty in answering these charges comes from one's definition of fundamentalism and one's understanding of its historical background and presuppositions. A second difficulty comes from the theological presuppositions which the examiner himself brings into his investigation. Generally, this second factor plays a very large role in contemporary criticism. One would expect Emil Brunner to criticize fundamentalism, since he has no sympathy for one of the basic doctrines of fundamentalism—faith in an infallible Bible. And when one remembers the leading part Dr. C. C. Kim has played in introducing liberal higher criticism into the Korean church, one can also understand his critical reactions to fundamentalism. The deeply Barthian sympathies of Dr. Rhee Jong-sung are also evident in Korea and in his critical starting-point. These men are guided more by their neo-liberal tendencies than by historical fairness. There may also be some confusion between that aspect of fundamentalism which was evident before the 1930's and the aspect which has flowered more recently (which we choose to call neo-fundamentalism).

In its widest sense, fundamentalism may simply be regarded as one more name for the historic Christian faith, the defense and propagation of the supernatural gospel.[5] And, in that sense, it is often more popularly called con-

---

4. Rhee Jong-sung, "Trends of Modern Theology," *Theological Forum* V (Seoul: Yonsei University, 1959), 85 ff.
5. J. Gresham Machen, *Christianity and Liberalism* (Grand Rapids: Eerdmans Publishing Co., 1946), remains the most authoritative doctrinal statement of the differences between liberalism and classic Christianity.

servatism in Asia or evangelicalism in Britain and Europe.[6]

However, as a specific historical movement, fundamentalism has a narrower meaning. As a historical phenomenon, it was a uniquely American twentieth century expression of Christianity. By the end of the nineteenth century, the power of theological liberalism (or what Machen preferred to call naturalism) was beginning to be felt strongly in the schools and churches of the United States. Originating in Germany and England, liberalism was born out of the rationalism of the Enlightenment movement. It created distrust in the objective revelation and infallible authority of the Bible. It questioned such items of doctrine as the virgin birth of Christ, His deity, His substitutionary atonement for sinners, His physical resurrection, and His physical return in glory. Liberal critics of the Old Testament questioned the Mosaic authorship of the Pentateuch and thereby the traditional chronological order as stated in the Bible itself. An evolutionary concept of Israel's religion was applied to the chronological order of Law, Psalms, and Prophets, and a new arrangement appeared of Prophets, Law, and Psalms.[7] The New Testament was also attacked. Men questioned the accuracy of the gospel records, the authorship of many of the Pauline letters. Later dates were assigned to the books, thus attacking the credibility of the Bible-claimed authors. Whenever the critic did not want to accept a passage, it was stated that a later writer, known as a redactor, had made the change.

Coupled with these theological attacks were scientific attacks as well. Charles Darwin's theory of evolution, developed in the nineteenth century, began to be used to discredit the historic and biblical view of man and the world.[8]

6. This is the usage one finds in James I. Packer, *Fundamentalism and the Word of God* (London: Inter-Varsity Fellowship, 1958).
7. Herbert F. Hahn, *The Old Testament in Modern Research* (Philadelphia: Fortress Press, 1966), pp. 1 ff.
8. Norman Furniss, *The Fundamentalist Controversy, 1918–1931* (Hamden, Conn.: Archon Books, 1963), pp. 76 ff.

Man could now be pictured as, not depraved and fallen, but as progressing to perfection. The necessity for the supernatural became less apparent, as science could be used to explain more of what we do not understand. So-called "miracles" could now be explained from a non-supernatural point of view.

In the face of such criticism, fundamentalism arose to reassert certain essentials or fundamentals of the Christian faith. Though in some sense a protest movement, its protests were against the negativism and destructiveness of liberal criticism. Counter-action might be a more fitting expression to designate its early efforts.

Aware that American seminaries, Christian publishers, and denominational posts of leadership were being surrendered to liberalism, it countered with annual Bible conferences, mass evangelism, the erection of conservative Bible schools and seminaries and foreign mission boards, and a new emphasis on preaching and missions.[9] In 1909, a series of twelve volumes entitled *The Fundamentals* began to appear, representing the wide interests of the defenders of supernatural Christianity.[10] A total of ninety articles was written for the series, twenty-nine devoted to the question of biblical authority. The spirit of the work was typical of the spirit of early fundamentalism—calm, determined, intending merely the reaffirmation of fundamental truths.[11]

Doctrinally, a great many elements were part of this early fundamentalism. The sweep of its campaign brought together Calvinists and Arminians, Baptists and Presbyterians. Dispensationalists were also strong leaders in the program. One recent author has identified the writers of

---

9. Ronald Nash, *The New Evangelicalism* (Grand Rapids: Zondervan Publishing House, 1963), pp. 21-29.
10. Recently edited, complete in two volumes, as *The Fundamentals for Today*, ed. by Charles L. Feinberg (Grand Rapids: Kregel Publications, 1958).
11. Ernest R. Sandeen, *The Roots of Fundamentalism* (Chicago: University of Chicago Press, 1970), pp. 188 ff.

thirty-one of the ninety articles appearing in the series as adherents of dispensationalism.[12] The diversity of theological background was astonishing. A common liberal foe kept them at peace throughout the nineteenth and early twentieth centuries.

As the battle between Christianity and liberalism was pressed within denominational circles, divisions began to occur. In the Northern Presbyterian and Baptist churches the debate led to schisms. Formerly professor of New Testament at Princeton Seminary, J. Gresham Machen, a Presbyterian, was disciplined along with others like Carl McIntire for refusing to separate themselves from the fundamentalist-supported Independent Board for Presbyterian Foreign Missions (created to provide an honestly Presbyterian board).[13] In 1936, Machen and one hundred ministers left to form the Presbyterian Church of America.[14] Similar actions took place in the attack on liberalism in the Northern Baptist Convention. *leads to GAR*

It should not be hard to see now why fundamentalism remains a subject of criticism by liberal and neo-liberal scholars. What is surprising is the large amount of criticism heaped on the movement by those who wish to be identified with its basic thrust as a champion of biblical truths. Particularly strong is the criticism of men like Carl F. H. Henry and other representatives of the so-called neo-evangelical movement.[15] It has prompted an equally vehement defense of fundamentalism and a correlative attack on neo-evangelicalism by men like Carl McIntire. What attitude should Calvinism show in this raging debate?

---

12. *Ibid.*, pp. 199-203.
13. Edwin H. Rian, *The Presbyterian Conflict* (Grand Rapids: Eerdmans Publishing Co., 1940), pp. 127 ff. Rian's account is very sympathetic to the movement.
14. Lefferts Loetscher, *The Broadening Church* (Philadelphia: University of Pennsylvania Press, 1957), pp. 148 ff.
15. Cf. Carl F. H. Henry, *Evangelical Responsibility in Contemporary Theology* (Grand Rapids: Eerdmans Publishing Co., 1957), pp. 32 ff.

116

(1.) Though we may be justifiably critical of many features of fundamentalism as a historical movement, these criticisms should not cloud our basic agreement with fundamentalism's firm stand on the side of scriptural theology and the historic Christian faith. Machen himself had theological difficulties in being identified with many fundamentalist-oriented programs but, while "not precisely described as a fundamentalist at all," was willing nevertheless to be recognized as a champion of fundamentalism, in terms of its devotion to the Christianity of the Bible.[16] The fear of McIntire and others, expressed in their strong criticism of neo-evangelicalism, would seem to come in part from their fear that much contemporary criticism by conservatives is pressing too unfairly the negations and novelties of fundamentalism, while stressing too little their common bond in the central and indispensable core of Christian faith. There are many virtues to the argument.

(2.) At the same time, there may be some virtue also in speaking of the later stages of fundamentalism (particularly after the 1930's) as distinct enough in temperament and program to merit a name distinct enough to separate its emphasis from the early fundamentalism. Perhaps neo-fundamentalism could describe this later stage as effectively as any other phrase. In line with this suggestion, the criticism of neo-evangelicalism may be more a criticism of neo-fundamentalism than of fundamentalism. And the vigorous defense of fundamentalism by men like Carl McIntire may be misunderstood because he does not seem as willing to recognize any differences significant enough to differentiate the movement called fundamentalism from a movement which might be called neo-fundamentalism.

(3.) This neo-fundamentalist stage has amplified some of the danger spots in early fundamentalism, what Carl Henry calls "the fundamentalist reduction."[17] Machen (and

16. Ned B. Stonehouse, *J. Gresham Machen: A Biographical Memoir* (Grand Rapids: Eerdmans Publishing Co., 1955), pp. 336 ff.
17. Henry, *loc. cit.*

his colleagues at Westminster Seminary) also feared pietistic novelties and perfectionist vagaries and distinguished within fundamentalism between biblical Christianity and certain excrescences.[18] Fundamentalism, as a word, was not big enough in its scope to define his faith. As he wrote once to the fledgling Bryan University, "Thoroughly consistent Christianity, to my mind, is found only in the Reformed or Calvinistic Faith; and consistent Christianity, I think, is the Christianity easiest to defend."

4. Because fundamentalism was a theological amalgamation of some widely diversified views, it tended to promote lack of concern for precise formulation of Christian doctrine, "an intentional moratorium on discussing doctrinal differences. The result was little mutual devotion to the dedicated enterprise of theological study and research."[19]

5. Through the influences of pietism and dispensationalism, the fundamentalist movement tended to narrow "the whole counsel of God" and not to relate the Christian revelation to cultural and social life. We do not mean to say that fundamentalism had no concern to exhibit Christianity as a world-and-life view.[20] But the danger of reducing the Christian faith to one of personal piety exclusively was a real one, felt especially keenly by those early leaders who moved in Calvinistic circles.

6. Fundamentalism's biblical demand for discipline against unbelief in the church, and its biblical call for the purity of the church, carried with it the danger of perversion into an unbiblical negativism and independency. Unfortunately, that danger, though not implicit in a call for separation, became reality in certain areas of fundamentalism in the years following the 1930's.

---

18. Stonehouse, *op. cit.*, p. 337.
19. Henry, *op. cit.*, p. 34.
20. One finds such a concern in Carl F. H. Henry, *The Uneasy Conscience of Modern Fundamentalism* (Grand Rapids: Eerdmans Publishing Co., 1947).

CHAPTER XVIII

NEO-FUNDAMENTALISM

The movement called fundamentalism in the early twentieth century in America was a group united around the proclamation and defense of biblical Christianity. But it was a union composed of very diversified elements. It had made allies of pietism and dispensationalism, Calvinism and Arminianism, episcopacy and independency. Especially in the decades immediately preceding World War II, those explosive elements, kept settled through struggle against a common foe, now began to bubble and grate against one another.[1] There were withdrawals and shifts. From it all came what might be called a new mixture, or at least, enough of a change in the combination of the old elements to produce another emphasis within "conservative" theology. That shift we choose to call neo-fundamentalism.

Several factors contributed to this change in the face of fundamentalism. Fundamentalism began to be more rigidly identified with dispensationalism. Dispensationalists themselves were willing to make this identification. In fact, some elements even were prone to label non-dispensationalists as incipient liberals.[2] This identification made the Calvinistic wing of the fundamentalist movement even more reluctant to associate themselves with the increasing shifts.

The fissure between dispensationalism and covenant the-

1. Erling Jorstad, *The Politics of Doomsday* (Nashville: Abingdon Press, 1970), pp. 21 ff.
2. Edward J. Carnell, *The Case for Orthodox Theology* (Philadelphia: Westminster Press, 1959), pp. 117-119.

ology was also helped considerably by an acrimonious debate among those conservative Presbyterians who had withdrawn from the northern Presbyterian Church to form a new denomination. Within the newly formed Presbyterian Church of America (one section later called the Bible Presbyterian Church), violent debate arose over such issues as Christian liberty, premillennialism, and dispensationalism.[3] Machen's colleagues at Westminster Seminary demanded strongly that dispensationalism be purged from the movement. Others, including Carl McIntire, insisted that the faculty members' "attack on dispensationalism" was ultimately an attack on premillennialism.[4] The outcome of the sad debate was another division, and the erection of what came to be called the Bible Presbyterian Church and the Orthodox Presbyterian Church. It also meant that one strong, balanced segment of the earlier fundamentalism, the Calvinism of the Old Princeton Seminary (and now Westminster Seminary), was aligning itself more and more against dispensational emphases. Two of the major forces in fundamentalism now were dividing increasingly.

With this increasing hesitancy of some Calvinistic elements to be classified as fundamentalists, one deterrent to fundamentalist novelties was removed and the dangers within earlier fundamentalism began to become more visible. What had earlier been merely possible danger now was becoming real weakness.

In addition, church divisions within the Presbyterian and Baptist churches soured many conservatives who remained within the larger churches. These groups in turn now began to attack what they felt to be the "fundamentalist spirit of lovelessness and strife."[5] Fundamentalists responded to the

---

3. George Marsden, "Perspective on the Division of 1937," *Presbyterian Guardian* XXXIII (Jan.–April, 1964).
4. Stonehouse, *op. cit.*, pp. 503 ff.
5. Henry, *Evangelical Responsibility in Contemporary Theology, op. cit.*, p. 43.

charges and soon the theological conflict with liberalism was deteriorating into an attack of fundamentalist upon fundamentalist. The debate was moving from a biblical call for separation from unbelief to an unbiblical reactionary spirit. This spirit of criticism often deteriorated again into an unscholarly attack upon organizations and personalities not willing to align themselves with stipulated separatist movements. The call for separation becomes a call for separation not simply from unbelief but from those fundamentalists who could not share the neo-fundamentalist's vision. This demand has often been called "second-degree" or "third-degree separation," or just simply "separation."

From all of these elements came a new mood, a new temperament, what might best be called the neo-fundamentalist reduction (to borrow partly the language of Carl Henry). It is not exclusively an American movement, nor is it exclusively Western. One will find its characteristics in many areas and in many churches. Neo-fundamentalism will show itself in many ways—extreme dispensationalism; excessive emotionalism; social withdrawal; fear of cultural challenges to the gospel; neglect of ethical issues; theological pugnaciousness; pietistic individualism.

In particular, the following areas of neo-fundamentalism indicate some of the more prominent danger signs for which to look.

1. Along with earlier fundamentalism, neo-fundamentalism seeks to propagate and defend the gospel. But increasingly the emphasis on defense overpowers the emphasis on propagation. The mood moves from positive-negative to excessively negative, from warfare to pugnaciousness, from graciousness and courtesy to the vocabulary of invective, from movements to men.

2. Neo-fundamentalism, along with fundamentalism, speaks strongly for biblical Christianity, but it declares "an intentional moratorium on discussing doctrinal differences."

121

Calvinism's emphasis on the organic sweep of biblical theology, on the demands of the kingdom of Christ for all of life, are often relatively silent. As a result, neo-fundamentalism's emphasis tends to fall increasingly on isolated fundamentals, and there is reluctance to study those precise doctrinal formulations that may divide Calvinist from Arminian, or dispensationalist from Calvinist.

(3.) Neo-fundamentalism tends to show a strong pietistic emphasis on personal religious experience while, at the same time, a deemphasis on the social and cultural imperative of Christianity. Religion becomes restricted to the individual's life of prayer, Bible study, and church attendance—a part of life separated ordinarily from the problems raised by economics, sociology, and the natural sciences. As one acute critic has noted, "In ordinary life, they deal with their business, as though they can be neutral about it, while their Christian faith is kept in a separate compartment. . . . Most of them, however, have a dichotomy of thinking which enables them to regard the world and its affairs 'neutrally,' while in the sphere of religion they follow the traditional Christian lines."[6] So, in those neo-fundamentalist circles where Christian schools are founded, the school often becomes known more for what it does not teach than for what it does teach. The cultural sciences are not so much molded and guided by biblical theology as they are limited and restricted.[7]

(4.) Neo-fundamentalism's proper distrust of evolution often shifts to a distrust of science as well. And when it does not, it nevertheless "approaches science on the edge of an anti-evolutionary spirit, whereas a more positive and comprehensive outlook" shaped the earlier fundamentalist

---

6. W. Stanford Reid, "Modernism-Romanism-Fundamentalism-Calvinism," *Calvin Forum*, December, 1948, p. 88, quoted in Nash. *op. cit.*, p. 25.
7. Louis Gasper, *The Fundamentalist Movement* (The Hague: Mouton and Co., 1963), pp. 104-109.

attitude toward science. As Henry puts it, "Some fundamentalist popularizers boldly disparaged scientific studies as a whole, using sarcasm and ridicule to reinforce their deficiency of logic. . . . Some evangelicals in America requested of science only that it refrain from tampering with the reality of the supernatural, with the role of transcendent divine power in creating the graded levels of life and the essential uniqueness of man. . . . Nature as a divine laboratory in which men may read the plan and thought of God, and science as a sphere of divine vocation where Christian young people may facilitate the control of nature to man's purposes under God, were all but lost as motivating purposes."[8] The neo-fundamentalist interest in science had become mainly anti-evolutionary.

⑤ Neo-fundamentalism, along with earlier fundamentalism, seeks to point out liberalism in existing denominations and urges cooperation among conservatives. However, its promotion of rival interdenominational cooperation gravitates sometimes into antidenominationalism, or caustic criticism of even those fundamentalist denominations which do not feel they can join their organization for reasons of conscience. Such a line moves quickly from a call for repentance to a call for movements, or what might be called movementism. The American Council of Christian Churches, as it is interpreted to the public by Carl McIntire, is often cited by its opponents as bearing this image.[9] From such a perspective, neo-evangelicalism often becomes a favorite target for neo-fundamentalist criticism. Representatives of this movement are accused of making a subtle retreat to a compromised fundamentalism.

⑥ Neo-fundamentalism, along with earlier fundamentalism, puts much emphasis on the biblical doctrine of the church. (Many neo-evangelicals, on the contrary, say it

---

8. Henry, *op. cit.*, p. 42.
9. Gasper, *op. cit.*, pp. 23 ff.; Ralph Lord Roy, *Apostles of Discord* (Boston: Beacon Press, 1953), pp. 185 ff.

neglects this doctrine.[10]) In particular, there is a strong stress on the purity of the church, and on spiritual unity within the fundamentals of the gospel. However, neo-fundamentalism so stresses the invisible unity of the church that it virtually neglects the visible unity of the church and creates two churches—one visible and one invisible. For the neo-fundamentalist, biblical unity becomes a purely spiritual, invisible unity, and all obligations regarding the unity of the church are fulfilled by a simple nod toward the idea of invisible unity.

(7.) Neo-fundamentalism, along with earlier fundamentalism, had properly asserted that personal and social ethical problems cannot be solved ultimately without the supernatural rebirth of individuals through the work of the Holy Spirit (John 3:3, 5). And it expresses its social concern in such things as temperance movements, city rescue missions, hospitals, orphanages, and relief work for the poor of the world. But it often restricts its approach to personal ethics as merely abstinence from dubious social externals and does not probe deeper into Christian behavior patterns for the home, for work, for leisure. Its answers to contemporary problems of social ethics often descends to reductions into simple cliches or avoiding the problem by negation. The question of American racial tensions and civil rights is resolved by pointing out the communist exploitation of this problem. In fact, anti-communism is often a very strong feature of the approach of neo-fundamentalism to problems of social ethics.[11]

10. For examples of such neo-evangelical charges, cf. Henry, *op. cit.*, p. 35 ff.; Carnell, *op. cit.*, pp. 114-117, 132-137.
11. Jorstad, *op. cit.*, pp. 92-98.

CHAPTER XIX

NEO-EVANGELICALISM—ITS MESSAGE

In 1948, during the opening exercises of Fuller Theological Seminary, California, Dr. Harold Ockenga introduced a new word to the theological world—"neo-evangelicalism." The phrase was an attempt to relate this new phase of evangelical theology to the fundamentalism of the past, while at the same time emphasizing its dissatisfaction with some of that past.[1] A new word was needed to mark what Ockenga and others felt was going to be a new beginning for orthodoxy, a "fundamentalist renascence."

Since that day, the word and the movement behind it have reached large proportions in the United States and elsewhere. But, as it has expanded, so have its problems and its critics. In more recent years the movement seems less and less cohesive in certain theological areas (particularly the doctrine of Scripture).[2] To American critics like Carl McIntire and the circle of men often associated with the name of Bob Jones University, it is strongly condemned as "the new neutralism," "more dangerous than modernism or neo-orthodoxy."[3] To dispensationalists like Robert P. Lightner of Dallas Theological Seminary, it contains dangers centering around unrealistic optimism, doctrinal neglect,

---

1. Victor M. Matthews, *Neo-Evangelicalism* (Des Plaines, Ill.: Regular Baptist Press, 1971), pp. 1-2.
2. *Ibid.*, pp. 15 ff.
3. Charles Woodbridge, *The New Neutralism* (Greenville, S. C.: Bob Jones University Press, n.d.).

125

substituting for the essential, deflection to a powerless message, conceding too much, amalgamation with unbelief.[4] It is attacked for compromising the faith, appeasing evil, leaning toward neo-orthodoxy.

Like fundamentalism, neo-evangelicalism had its origin as a protest. However, in this case, the protest was as strongly directed against evangelical theology as against liberal theology. Carl F. H. Henry, former editor of *Christianity Today* and a founding father of the movement, had felt there had been a subtle shift from classic fundamentalism as a theology to fundamentalism as a negative reactionary spirit (what we have called neo-fundamentalism). This later stage, this neo-fundamentalism, was said to have discredited fundamentalism as a legitimate theological option. Henry and others knew that fundamentalism, as a faithful expression of classic Christianity, could not be abandoned. What they sought to abandon were those features which were not properly reflective of the true spirit of fundamentalism—"the lack of theological and historical perspective; vagueness of doctrinal formulations; neglect of scholarship; lack of relevant contemporary literature movement; antidenominationalism; identification with dispensationalism; neglect of Christianity's relationship to culture and society; reactionary negativism and strife; narrowing of the gospel to personal religious experience."[5]

At the same time, many within the new emphasis were also aware that neo-orthodoxy could not provide any better answer. As Ockenga, now president of Gordon-Conwell Divinity School, Massachusetts, put it in 1958, "Neo-evangelicalism breaks with neo-orthodoxy because it declares that it accepts the authority of the Bible . . . neo-evangelicalism breaks with the liberal in [its] embrace of

4. Robert P. Lightner, *Neo-Evangelicalism* (Des Plaines, Ill.: Regular Baptist Press, 1965), pp. 137 ff.
5. Nash, *op. cit.*, pp. 23-32.

the full orthodox system of doctrine against that which the modernist has accepted. . . ."[6]

Against this background, new centers of discussion began to emerge within Western evangelical circles in the 1940's and 1950's. Men like Carl Henry called for a fresh conservative recognition of social responsibility. Men like Gordon H. Clark pleaded for a "contemporary Christian literature that studies all phases of intellectual interest . . ."[7] philosophy, sociology science and politics. There was a growing shift away from dispensationalism, a more tolerant attitude toward varying views of eschatology. And particulary in three areas, there was rather obvious evidence of theological ferment and even inner disagreement within the neo-evangelical orbit.

Men like Bernard Ramm, now professor of systematic theology at California Baptist Seminary, began to call for a new examination of the relation between science and the Bible. Ramm himself offered such a reexamination in 1955, when his explosive book on that subject appeared.[8] Critical of what he terms "pedantic hypcrorthodoxy" and "fiat creationism," he points to God as "world ground."[9] "God as world ground means a spiritual universe, creation to consummation, heaven to earth, matter to spirit, animal to man, time to eternity. The *how* of Nature is supplied by science, but this *how* of Nature is but the manifestation of the *that* of God who is in all things."[10] Critical also of what he terms "theistic evolution," Ramm's answer to both extremes is what he calls "progressive creationism."[11] Over the mil-

---

6. Harold J. Ockenga, "The New Evangelicalism," *The Park Street Spire*, February, 1958, pp. 4-5.
7. Gordon Clark, "Preface," in Carl F. H. Henry, *Remaking the Modern Mind* (Grand Rapids: Eerdmans Publishing Co., c. 1946), p. 13.
8. Ramm, *Christian View of Science and Scripture, op. cit.*
9. *Ibid.*, p. 84.
10. *Ibid.*, pp. 108-109.
11. *Ibid.*, p. 113.

lions of years of geologic history, God has been, by sovereign command, creating higher and higher forms of life. This process begins with "the concept in the mind of God, the idea, the form, the plan, the purpose. . . . This is followed by a sovereign and fiat act of creation by God at the level of vacancy or null and void. . . . After this comes the process, or derivative creation. God creating fiatly and sovereignly outside of Nature now turns the task of creation over to the Holy Spirit who is inside Nature. The Spirit, the Divine Entelechy of Nature, knows what is the divine blueprint and through process working from the level of vacancy realizes the divine form of intention in Nature."[12] For many of us, this does (not) seem too far removed from "theistic evolution."[13] In 1959 the science debate became more exciting when Edward J. Carnell, also associated with the neo-evangelical movement and then president of Fuller Theological Seminary, introduced the term, "threshold evolution" into the discussion.[14] Carnell conceded that "while orthodoxy does not think that the evidence for human evolution is compelling, the evidence is sufficient to give pause. The verdict of paleontology cannot be dismissed by pious ridicule."[15] Carnell, with others, also was willing to postulate a pre-Adamic race structurally similar to modern man, but earlier in time and inferior in endowment.

Neo-evangelicalism also opened debate on the question of fellowship with non-conservative theologians. A growing willingness was expressed by many within the new emphasis to converse with liberal and dialectical theologians. Though many were sharply critical of the World Council of Churches' inclusivism and intolerance, they were also critical of what

---

12. *Ibid.*, p. 116.
13. For an excellent apologetic critique at this point, consult Cornelius Van Til, *The New Evangelicalism* (Philadelphia: Westminster Theological Seminary, unpublished paper, n.d.), pp. 15 ff.
14. Carnell, *op. cit.*, pp. 92 ff.
15. *Ibid.*, p. 95.

they felt to be the exclusivism and intolerance of the International Council of Christian Churches.[16] What is a proper perspective? According to one sympathetic commentator, the neo-evangelical consensus on this question called for theological dialogue with liberals (without compromise); an evangelical attempt to define what might be called biblical ecumenicity; an evangelical critique of the existing ecumenical movements; a deeper program of evangelical cooperation.[17] The evangelistic campaigns of Billy Graham, the 1966 Berlin Congress on Evangelism can be cited as concrete examples of the application of these principles.

Particularly in this area, the arguments of Edward Carnell have been very acrid, especially in his sharp criticism of what he calls Machen's "separatism." Carnell attacked the great leader of Calvinism for not properly honoring the doctrine of the church, and thus allegedly planting the seeds of anarchy by encouraging separation from the church without proper grounds.[18] Carnell's views in particular have drawn heavy attack from not only neo-fundamentalist[19] and fundamentalist,[20] but even neo-evangelical[21] and Calvinistic[22] circles. Naturally those who consider Carnell as a representative spokesman for neo-evangelicalism thereby condemn the whole movement in condemning him. This view of Carnell as a typical representative seems difficult to believe in view of even the neo-evangelical criticism of his views.

The most critical center of debate opened up by neo-evangelicals has been the authority and inerrancy of Scripture. And again, the views of Carnell have been a center of

16. Millard Erickson, *The New Evangelical Theology* (Westwood, N. J.: Fleming H. Revell Co., 1968), pp. 41-43.
17. Nash, *op. cit.*, pp. 102-105.
18. Carnell, *op. cit.*, pp. 114-117.
19. Woodbridge, *loc cit.*
20. Lightner, *op. cit.*, pp. 95-100.
21. Nash, *op. cit.*, pp. 88-91.
22. Van Til, *op. cit.*, pp. 10-12.

much agitation. Though Carnell himself insisted, in the subsequent furor over his position, that he always has believed the inerrancy of Scripture, his criticisms of many of the viewpoints of B. B. Warfield and classic conservative theology, his admission of "seeming disharmonies" in the Old Testament histories,[23] made many dubious of Carnell's final standpoint in this issue. Again, those who regard Carnell as typical of neo-evangelical sentiment naturally condemn the whole movement with him.

Even assuming, however, that Carnell's views in this area may be to the left of the neo-evangelical center, one must still admit that neo-evangelicalism more and more seems to be widening a gap between inspiration and inerrancy.[24] This tendency has become especially pronounced in the last decade. To many neo-evangelicals, inspiration and inerrancy are not equivalent concepts. This may not necessarily mean (as some have interpreted it) that the neo-evangelical is denying the inerrancy of Scripture. There are many who feel it is necessary purely for clarification to keep inspiration separate from inerrancy. Ronald Nash seems typical of this standpoint.[25] On the other hand, Harold Lindsell, presently editor of *Christianity Today*, has commented that, in the more recent 1960's, "there are those who have been numbered among the new evangelicals, some of whom possess the keenest minds, who have broken, or are in the process of breaking, with the doctrine of an inerrant scripture."[26] Dr. Lindsell, speaking as a neo-evangelical himself, predicts a dangerous future for those who hold such a weak view of Scripture.

Where this shift eventually will lead to is, of course, difficult to say now. But its growing base cannot be denied.

---

23. Carnell, *op. cit.*, pp. 97-110.
24. Matthews, *op. cit.*, pp. 15-30.
25. Nash, *op. cit.*, pp. 75-77.
26. Harold Lindsell, "A Historian Looks at Inerrancy," *Bulletin of the Evangelical Theological Society* (Winter, 1965), 3-12.

"One observes with amazement and with sorrow that in the very orthodox circles where the twentieth-century battle for biblical authority has been most courageously fought, voices are being raised against the inerrancy of Holy Writ. Biblical Seminary in New York, an evangelical center where brilliant pioneering techniques of inductive Bible study were developed, saw in 1963, publication of Dewey M. Beegle's *The Inspiration of Scripture*, in which that faculty member —having embraced Neo-Orthodox, dialectic presuppositions as to the nature of truth—imposes them on Scripture, denies its inerrancy, and makes the incredible claim that evangelicals by a 'mental readjustment' can now retain inspiration without inerrancy and thereby rejoin mainline Protestant-ecumenical theology. North Park Seminary in Chicago, long known for its uncompromising free-church orthodoxy and piety, is now characterized by an anti-inerrancy approach to the Bible that finds Scripture truth-value not in any historical soundness or factual consistency possessed by the Word, but in its ability to trigger spiritual experience. Concordia Seminary, St. Louis, a bastion of biblical orthodoxy in the days of Theodore Engelder and W. F. Arndt, has in the last decade weakened its stand considerably. . . . And in many quarters of the American evangelical scene, from East coast to West, theologians who should be testifying to Scripture's total truth are preferring to avoid the word 'inerrancy,' are making no efforts to explain apparent discrepancies in the Bible, and are redefining 'truth' so that the Scripture can—we are confidently told— retain its absolute revelational veracity without de facto historical accuracy."[27]

27. John Warwick Montgomery, "Guest Editorial," *Bulletin of the Evangelical Theological Society* (Autumn, 1965), 125-126.

CHAPTER XX

NEO-EVANGELICALISM—ITS FAILURE

Neo-evangelicalism, as a mood, a temper, is not strictly an English-language phenomenon. Life in the area of the "younger churches" has been touched by the same subjectivism of neo-orthodoxy, and the same vagaries and gaudy extremes of neo-fundamentalism that prompted the rise of neo-evangelicalism on the American continent and in Europe. And so, one can hear in these places also the same calls for purification of evangelical thinking that we have come to call, rightly or wrongly, "neo-evangelicalism."

As in America and Europe, many of the world's evangelicals are sickened by the fear that fundamentalism is no longer a world-changing faith but a world-escaping fear. They are saddened by the lack of orthodox scholarship in academic circles.[1] There is fear that one of the reasons for a crippled evangelical literature movement may be conservative anti-intellectualism. There is fear that one of the reasons for a lack of a dedicated, respected body of scholars is evangelical neglect of Christianity's relationship to society and culture. So the call issues for an indigeneous theology.[2] Along with these fears, there is also the desire to recapture denominational leadership, rather than abandon these denominations to the forces of contemporary liberalism. The world evangelical courts opportunities to

---

1. The Second Asia Evangelical Consultation of Theological Education, *Report and Minutes* (Singapore, June 8-12, 1971), p. 17.
2. *Ibid.*, pp. 16 ff.

132

enter into written and oral dialogue with neo-orthodox theologians, remembering the dangers to the purity of their testimony but remembering also the challenge of an opportunity for their testimony.

In this same spirit, the world evangelical acknowledges his neglect of society and now seeks to find ways to make Christianity "in the third world" the mainspring of social reforms that it has been in some countries and that it ought to be in others.[3] Though these men do not openly use the word "neo-evangelical" (it seems to be a very new word in our world vocabulary), much of their emphases can be called "neo-evangelical" in tone.

What shall we say about this tone? It is condemned wholesale by Carl McIntire and other neo-fundamentalists. The neo-evangelical is often labelled as coming close to being "a half-hearted heretic," and the movement is condemned as "born of compromise, nurtured on pride of intellect, growing on the appeasement of evil, and doomed by the judgment of God's word."[4] Others, like Robert Lightner of Dallas Theological Seminary, are far more gracious, though still critical in spirit.

A warning against the dangers of easy generalization may be especially apt in discussing this issue. Lightner, an informed critic of neo-evangelicalism, writes these wise words. "Since such a wide range of divergence exists within neo-evangelicalism, it would be unwise to attempt to speak for them all. Some who are pleased to be designated 'neo-evangelicals' have more affinity to either neo-liberalism, neo-orthodoxy or fundamentalism than others. Some are to the right of center and others to the extreme left of center."[5] Lightner wrote those remarks as a preface to his

3. Dennis Clark, *The Third World and Mission* (Waco, Texas: Word Books, 1971), pp. 95 ff.

4. William Ashbrook, "The New Evangelicalism—The New Neutralism," *Central Conservative Baptist Quarterly* (Summer, 1959).

5. Robert P. Lightner, *The Saviour and the Scriptures* (Philadelphia: Presbyterian and Reformed Publishing Co., 1966), p. 147.

treatment of certain weak views of Scripture within the neo-evangelical circle. He adds, "These views are not shared by all, but they are shared by too many." Lightner's commentary seems especially pertinent in view of the neo-fundamentalist's tendency to see everything as black or white, and to fear any new theological developments as suspicious drifts toward unbelief.

In connection with this, and in view of the wide divergences within "neo-evangelicalism," the wisest thing may be to admit that "neo-evangelicalism" is not so much a movement as a mood, a temperament more than a theology, a disposition more than a theological position. As even some neo-evangelicals admit, the term is a misnomer and somewhat misleading. Its very vagueness invites denunciations from those who often call it "a subtle retreat to a compromised fundamentalism." The term had some usefulness in the 1940's and 1950's to describe the "fundamentalist renaissance" of that time. However, there have been continued changes since those days and the word may not be fully descriptive of some of the new twists and turns in the world right of the theological center.

In any case, one cannot simply condemn completely much of what the movement has stood for in the past. For example, the influence of classic Calvinism on many of the early leaders played a large part in some of the emphases of "neo-evangelicalism." Bernard Ramm, though a Baptist, was deeply influenced by the writings of Abraham Kuyper. Gordon Clark, who himself may no longer want to be completely identified with the movement, is a minister of the Reformed Presbyterian Church, Evangelical Synod. Carl F. H. Henry, the movement's loudest voice, dedicated one of his earlier books to Gordon Clark, Cornelius Van Til, and Harry Jellema. The neo-evangelical call for the penetration of the gospel into society, into education, into culture, is a call Calvinism has been making for many years. The fear of neo-fundamentalist anti-intellectualism is a fear

Calvinists have long drawn attention to. The neo-evangelical attack on neo-fundamentalism's reduction of Christianity and religion to a separate compartment of life is an attack Calvinism has been making for some time. As we have noted in an earlier chapter, Machen, often identified with fundamentalism, never felt that that word alone was sufficient to describe fully his views. He much preferred the term "Calvinism."

Even today, the Calvinist finds himself in deep sympathy with much of the neo-evangelical emphasis—the call for a Christian message that will not seek to solve all social problems by merely asserting that salvation alone is the answer; a search for Christian principles to apply to economics, sociology, and the natural sciences; a more constructive attitude toward science and philosophy; the encouragement of the scholarly defense of Christianity; a more tolerant attitude toward varying views of eschatology and a shift away from so-called dispensationalism; a condemnation of neo-fundamentalism's "fissiparous tendencies"; the rightness of Christians seeking to make "a friendly approach to those whom they are seeking to reach for Christ."[6]

At the same time, there are problems which neo-evangelicalism has not solved, and there are "points on which it seems that the new evangelicalism is in danger of compromising the Christian religion."[7]

1. Leaders within the neo-evangelical orbit have called for a reopening of the evangelical debate on the authority and inspiration of Scripture.[8] And, though any effort to study the Scriptures must be encouraged, the course of this new debate has not been altogether profitable. Some like Ramm and Carnell deal extensively with the relation of science and Scripture and leave the impression that the

6. Van Til, *op. cit.*, p. 4.
7. *Loc. cit.*
8. Carnell, *op. cit.*, pp. 109-110.

135

Bible is to be interpreted in the light of science and not science in the light of the Bible. Others, like Klaas Runia, are now distinguishing between inspiration and authority in pointed contrast to a position like that of B. B. Warfield, while at the same time insisting apparently on a verbal inspiration that leaves the Bible free from all error.[9] Still others, like Ralph Earle[10] and Daniel P. Fuller,[11] distinguish sharply between inspiration and inerrancy, seeming to affirm inspiration but deny inerrancy. Lightner, for example, characterizes Fuller's view of inspiration as that which "makes certain that we have an authoritative record of all that God wanted to make known. But it was not God's intention or purpose to secure inerrancy in peripheral matters. 'Peripheral matters' include Scriptural data which have nothing to do with faith and life, such as minor historical details, grammatical constructions and the like."[12] Carnell's views on Scripture have been interpreted frequently as belonging to this latter category. Others may not speak with the strength that Carnell uses but nevertheless express some hesitancy to stress total or complete inerrancy.

2. Leaders within the neo-evangelical circles have demanded consideration for the study of ecclesiology. In particular, they have called for a new look at the question of fellowship and separation. When should a believer leave a church which condones liberal teaching? Can a believer have fellowship across denominational lines? On what basis can he have fellowship? What should be the Christian's attitude toward the World Council of Churches?

These are not easy questions to solve, and we must be grateful that neo-evangelicalism has drawn our attention to

---

9. Runia, *op. cit.*, pp. 181-188.

10. Ralph Earle, "Further Thoughts on Biblical Inspiration," *Bulletin of the Evangelical Theological Society* (Winter, 1963), 7-17.

11. Daniel P. Fuller, "Benjamin B. Warfield's View of Faith and History," *Bulletin of the Evangelical Theological Society* (Spring, 1968), 78-83.

12. Lightner, *op. cit.*, pp. 82-83.

them. But we must also note that neo-evangelicalism has yet to provide a clear answer to them. Especially in recent years it has, in fact, shown ever more willingness than before to collaborate with liberals on an "equal partners" type of theological dialogue. The danger here, as Professor John Sanderson of Covenant College has indicated, is that "of absorbing Liberalism's attitudes, at the cost of losing the sharp edge of evangelicalism's basic beliefs."[13] No opportunity presented for discussions with the neo-liberal can be seized if it involves, with it, a compromise of theological purity. It is sometimes not easy to keep this balance. But it is a balance one can endanger without putting both feet on the wrong side of the line.[14]

3. Neo-evangelicals have called for an investigation of the relation between science and Scripture. But until now, the results have not been either uniform or always profitable. In particular, Ramm's efforts at harmonization have been criticized in many areas as an effort to subject Scripture to science. Some, like John C. Whitcomb, have labelled such views a "double revelation theory." According to this theory God is said to give to man two revelations of truth, Scripture and nature, "each of which is fully authoritative in its own realm: the revelation of God in Scriptures and the revelation of God in nature. . . . The theologian is the God-appointed interpreter of Scripture and the scientist is the God-appointed interpreter of nature, and each has specialized tools for determining the true meaning of the particular book of revelation which he is called upon to study."[15] The end result, argues Whitcomb, is a type of approach which leaves such questions as the origin of the universe, man, the magnitude of the flood, etc., to the scientist to solve, and

---

13. John W. Sanderson, Jr., "Neo-Evangelicalism and Its Critics," *The Sunday School Times* (Jan. 28, 1961), 82.
14. Van Til, *op. cit.*, pp. 23-30.
15. John C. Whitcomb, "Biblical Inerrancy and the Double Revelation Theory," *Grace Journal* (Winter, 1963), 3-20.

not the theologian. The theory closes the door to a biblical look at science's domain.

Though Whitcomb does not use the language in his analysis, it would not be hard to superimpose the old Kantian categories onto this "double revelation theory" and say that ultimately it is advocating that the noumenal cannot investigate the domain of the phenomenal. The total position in any final sense cannot therefore work out "a truly Christian philosophy of scientific methodology" until it challenges "the false metaphysical foundations that underlie so much of modern scientific methodology," foundations which seem to be assumed in the neo-evangelical's view of the revelation between the Bible and science. "If science is to do its work it needs the presuppositions which the Bible alone can give it. . . ."[16]

In view of the confused metaphysical basis for this new evangelical analysis and openness to science, many fear properly it may bring a new openness to evolution. Carnell's advocacy of what he has called "threshold evolution" has been attacked, though perhaps without full understanding of Carnell's use of the terms. But, however one may interpret Carnell's exposition, the difficulty, as Carl Henry has pointed out, is "that these phrases contribute to a verbal illusion which attracts the interest of the contemporary evolutionist somewhat under false pretenses. . . ." Carnell's employment of conventional scientific phrases with a contrary intention "therefore runs needless apologetic hazards."

4. Neo-evangelicals call for a firm response to social needs and a biblical social ethics. To many neo-fundamentalists, this sounds like a return to the social gospel, and it is strongly denounced as such.[17] Such criticism, however, seems overextended to say the least. Carl F. H. Henry, who has written very fully on this very theme, gives no indication

---

16. Van Til, *op. cit.*, p. 21.
17. Jorstad, *op. cit.*, p. 159.

of neglecting the individual application of the gospel or of replacing saints with philanthropists.

At the same time, neo-evangelicalism still runs the risk of measuring its social responsibilities in terms of its individual responsibilities. Many, particularly in Calvinistic circles, attack the neo-cvangelical proposals for social action as a "mod form" of pietism, which ignores the nature of the church as a communal body of Christ, demanding the communal answer of the people of God to problems of labor, education, government, and business.[18]

5. Neo-evangelicalism does not offer an apologetic completely consistent with the self-authenticating Christ. Ronald Nash sees well enough that the major figures in the movement—Carl F. H. Henry, Edward Carnell, Bernard Ramm—have a common thrust to much of what they say. But whether this can best be designated "presuppositionalism," whether you can associate the name of Cornelius Van Til with these men, and whether they finally represent a defense of Christianity "made on different grounds than that typified by the eighteenth- and nineteenth-century approaches made by Butler, Paley and others"[19] are assumptions difficult to defend.

On the one hand, all these men assert the importance of starting with God, want to reject the "natural theology" assumptions of neo-Thomism, want to emphasize the role faith plays, even in modern scientific naturalism. Nevertheless, as Van Til has stated repeatedly in distancing himself from these men,[20] they accept, with these principles, an emphasis on "the law of non-contradiction" (Carnell) or "logic as an exercise of the reason to test for truth" (Gordon Clark) or what Van Til designates as "Greek theism" (Carl

18. Bernard Zylstra, "Dr. Henry, Duality and Ethics," *Torch and Trumpet* XV, 5 (May–June, 1965), 19-21.

19. Nash, *op. cit.*, pp. 113-114.

20. Cf. C. Van Til, *The Case for Calvinism* (Philadelphia: Presbyterian and Reformed Publishing Co., 1963), pp. 61-105.

Henry) as one of their operating categories or presuppositions. And precisely here lies the basic weakness of this sort of apologetics. "It is the attempt to join higher forms of non-Christian thought in their opposition to lower forms of non-Christian thought in order that, to go on to something still higher and [different] than even the highest forms of non-Christian thought offer. The difficulty with this method is that the highest forms of non-Christian thought rest upon the same foundation as the lowest forms of non-Christian thought. This foundation is man as would be self-existent and self-explanatory. The highest forms, no less than the lower forms of non-Christian thought, assume that the world and man are not created by God but exist by Chance. If this were true then the principles of logical reasoning by means of which man is supposed to construct the argument for the existence of his god, are themselves products of chance. On this basis the law of contradiction would itself be a product of chance. The entire idea of 'systematic coherence' would be meaningless."[21]

21. Van Til., *The New Evangelicalism*, p. 62.

Chapter XXI

THE REFORMED FAITH

Our pilgrimage through the world of theology has taken us from demythologization to neo-evangelicalism. And now we come to the end of the road and what some call "the Reformed faith" and others call "Calvinism." Where have we arrived?

Originally the word "Reformed" characterized those churches in the sixteenth century which rose to protest the errors and abuses which were dominating the Roman Catholic Church of the Middle Ages. In a broad sense, the term was applicable to all the churches of the Reformation, for they all professed but one aim: to live by the Word of God, both in the wide sphere of the life of the church and in the private sphere of the life of the individual believer.[1]

More recently, the term has a more restricted meaning. It is usually identified in theology with five points of doctrine: total depravity, unconditional election, limited atonement, irresistible grace, perseverance of the saints. In the fullest sense, this restriction of the term is truly no restriction at all. For these points of doctrine were hammered out in a theological debate which sought to define the very heart of the gospel—the meaning of grace. They were formulated by the famous Synod of Dordt in the Netherlands, over 350 years ago. And the center of the discussion at Dordt was not some minor difference of emphasis. The question

1. Klaas Runia, "Is It Still Worthwhile to Be Reformed Today," II, *Torch and Trumpet* XX, 6 (June, 1970), 9.

was more basic: what is final in man's salvation—God's grace or man's work of faith? The five points of Dordt were spokes on the wheel that all radiated from the hub—grace.[2]

In the world of theology today, this biblical call of sovereign grace is being challenged again from two diverse directions. On the one hand, in the country where the Synod of Dordt convened, and at one of the academic citadels of Calvinism, the Free University of Amsterdam, there seems to be some evidence of growing dissatisfaction with this thought-pattern of Dordt. Dr. G. C. Berkouwer, though claiming to seek to retain the heart of Dordt, the "unmerited grace of God in the way of salvation, election as the fountain of salvation,"[3] wants to reject the entire causal framework employed by Dordt in which God is seen "as causing all things,"[4] and to substitute for it "a framework that does justice to the doxological intent of the canons."

In this same searching way, Berkouwer's more recent attitude toward Rome and toward Barthianism is increasingly less critical and more activistic in its thrust. The pattern of language has become so markedly different from his earlier writings that Cornelius Van Til can speak with force of "the earlier Berkouwer" and the "later Berkouwer." Of special concern to many has been Berkouwer's alleged shifts regarding the inspiration and authority of Scripture. "In his earlier work on Scripture Berkouwer said, in effect, that no fact of experience or history *can* arise which should force the reconsideration of the basic presupposition that only in the light of Scripture can any fact be seen for what it is. Today such a position as he formerly held is, in effect, said to be abstract and formal."[5]

But there is another threat to biblical Calvinism, repre-

---

2. Peter Y. DeJong, ed., *Crisis in the Reformed Churches* (Grand Rapids: Reformed Fellowship, Inc., 1968), pp. 52 ff.
3. G. C. Berkouwer, "Vragen Rondom de Belijdenis," *Gereformeerd Theologisch Tijdschrift* LXIII (1963), 1-41.
4. Van Til, *The Sovereignty of Grace*, p. 34.
5. *Ibid.*, p. 82.

senting, from another side of the pendulum, a further narrowing down, one step further from the heart. This is the Calvinism in the life of the "younger churches," the Calvinism not of Europe but of Africa and Asia. Here, under the influence of Western secularism's compartmentalization of religion from the ordinary matters of daily living, under the influence of Eastern asceticism and African messiahism where the religious life is restricted to one of hermit abstentions in some holy place hermetically sealed off from the so-called "evil, real" world, we are finding another challenge to the Reformed faith. In this new threat, the five points of Calvinism have moved from the status of road to the status of roadsign, from the place of action to the formula on which we act. The church becomes not the people of God, but a building, not a program of witness and service and worship, but an hour of singing and praying and preaching.

This new twist is not frequently called Calvinism or the Reformed faith. It is more often called conservative theology. And perhaps that designation is more accurate.

Conservative theology, as the "younger church" situation has defined it, is often institutionalized, bureaucratic theology. It is also isolated theology. It changes John's demand for separation from the world (I John 2:15-17) into McIntire's demand for separation from those who do not separate from those who have not separated. It becomes isolated from the future by consolidation with the past; hesitates to engage in creative theology because of its proper fear of destructive critical theology; fears the left wing and the right wing and so remains on dead center; discusses theology rather than lives theology; puts the cosmic dynamic of the kingdom of God into storage by limiting God's rule to the future exclusively.

Conservative theology, as the situation of "the younger churches" has refined it, is defensive theology. It guards rather than promotes, retrenches rather than advances, commands by word rather than by example. What does it

143

leave us? Preaching without large vision and reforming conviction; leadership from the politicians instead of from the prophets; revivals without reformation; $10,000 church buildings with $1 programs; disillusioned college students who are dropping out of the "church world"; people trying to find God's grace from special emotional experiences rather than from God's Word; congregations showing their emptiness and dissatisfaction through lack of support for the church's institutions.

Where shall we go? Is it still worthwhile to be Reformed today? Or is "conservative" a better road? Or shall we move to the other end of the spectrum, to the "neo-Calvinism" of G. C. Berkouwer?

The Reformed faith is still a word that can be meaningful for a world theology. Our clash with modern theology in this guidebook should have indicated that by now. As Klaas Runia has said, "Nearly all modern theologies are to some extent (sometimes even to a large extent) based on one or another philosophical system. Although they proclaim that the Bible gives the answer to our deepest human questions, these theologies often do not let the Bible speak for itself. The Bible is squeezed into the straitjacket of preconceived opinions and ideas. . . . Over against all this, we can merely say: we want to be 'Reformed.' That is to say, we want to build our faith on the Word of God as we find this in the Bible. It is not in our freedom to do with this Bible what pleases us. We may not lord it over the Bible, but the Bible is lord of our life and thinking. We must not tell Paul and John, Peter and James, Matthew and Luke, what the real message is, but we must be willing to be taught by them. Yes, here too we can only be 'Reformed.' For this term means nothing else than that God's Word, God's Word alone, is the absolute and final authority in matters of faith and conduct. . . ."[6]

---

6. Runia, *op. cit.*, 10.

Our clash with liberal theology (even evangelical theology) has also indicated that modern man means more by theology than merely textbook doctrine. When modern man talks about theology, he often talks about politics, education, economics, labor unionism, revolutions. Theology has become a very comprehensive term in today's world. Can the Reformed faith cope with it? "Conservative" theology certainly cannot.

One scholar wrote these words about the sixteenth century Reformation movement under Calvin: "Calvin's theology was more or less directly responsible for the Scottish uprising, the revolt of the Netherlands, the French wars of religion, and the English civil war. It was Calvin's doctrine of the state as a servant of God that established the idea of constitutional government and led to the explicit acknowledgement of the rights and liberties of subjects, and, in due course, to tolerance. These facts reveal Calvin as, in effect, the producer . . . of some of the most fundamental ingredients of post-Renaissance western civilization. It is doubtful whether any other theologian has ever played so significant a part in world history."[7] That sounds like comprehensive theology, doesn't it? Where is the Calvin of the twentieth century world?

The Reformed faith operated in sixteenth century Europe, and operates in the twentieth century world, from what Dr. Calvin Seerveld of Trinity Christian College, Chicago, has called "three biblical givens." Without them, we can merely have a faith that "conserves." What are they?

1. The church is not a collection of individual members, but one body, the body of Christ, the people of God, the fellowship of the Spirit. No Christian is all by himself when he embraces the saving work of Christ by faith. He is

---

7. Cf. W. Stanford Reid, "The Impact of Calvinism on Sixteenth Century Europe," *International Reformed Bulletin*, No. 31 (Oct., 1967), 3-10.

grafted into the body of Christ, symbolically initiated and sealed into it by baptism.

(2) The life of the church in the New Testament was a full-orbed, total life. The church of Acts 2 and 4 sounds almost like a commune, with their fellowship of voluntarily shared material possessions, abiding by the rule of the apostles, who sought to keep order among the more than 3,000 members. As the new Israel, their "worship" took place within the rainbow-rich field of many other faith-shaped activities.

(3) Spiritual life was far more than what went on within the walls of a building for an hour on Sunday morning. It was manifest in lives so overpowered by the Holy Spirit that they became living letters of Jesus Christ (II Cor. 3:3). It was the kingdom life of the Spirit, the rule of God translated by the indwelling of the Holy Spirit into tangibles like righteousness, peace, and joy (Rom. 14:17). It was a "program of God," centered in the redemptive work of Jesus Christ, with cosmic dimensions to touch every part of life for Christ.[8]

None of this means some No-church movement after the fashion of Watchman Nee or Uchimura. But it does mean preaching "the whole counsel of God" (Acts 20:28). It means preaching the kingship of Christ, the rule of God, that all life belongs to the Lord—not just "church" life, or even merely home life, personal life, school life. It means all societal life patterns and relationships.

This means Christian action as the body of Christ, an expression of the communion of the saints in the home, in education, in politics, in journalism, in art, in science. It may mean Christian schools and universities that can bear the cross of Christ in the lecture hall and the science lab.

---

8. Calvin Seerveld, et al., *Out of Concern for the Church* (Toronto: Wedge Publishing Foundation, 1970), p. 58. I have modified Dr. Seerveld's analysis of such ideas as the kingdom of God and the church, while seeking to retain his positive thrust.

It may mean Christian labor unions willing to bear the yoke of Christ (Matt. 11:29-30). It may mean Christian political life that seeks to do more than simply avoid corruption, that seeks to reform politics from its roots with the Word of God. It may mean Christian art institutes that shape clay and canvas in the light of the beauty of Christ's glory.

The Reformed faith does not stop with five points (or even fifty points). That is just the beginning. To make it the end produces the caricature we have designated "conservative" theology.

Which shall it be? Biblical Calvinism? Or "conservatism"?

INDEXES

I. Scripture References

150

II. Authors

151

Hwang, C. H., 47

Illich, I., 74

Jellema, W. H., 134
Jeremias, J., 26
Jones, D. G., 79
Jorstad, E., 119, 124, 138

Kan, H. B., x, 19, 27, 29, 36, 48, 87
Kant, I., 1, 2, 3, 4, 5, 6, 64, 70, 78, 100
Kierkegaard, S., 13, 15, 17
Kim, C. C., 112, 113
Klooster, F., 11, 21, 24, 25
Knox, R. A., 95, 104
Knudsen, R. D., 35
Koch, K., 66
Kraus, C. N., 107
Kuyper, A., 134

Leary, T., 94
Lee, R. J., 97
Lessing, G. E., 7ff
Lightner, R. P., 125, 126, 129, 133, 134, 136
Lindsell, H., 130
Loetscher, L., 116
Luther, M., 58

Machen, J. G., vii, 113, 114, 116, 118, 120, 135
Macquarrie, J., 35, 75, 81
Marsden, G., 120
Marx, K., 64, 67
Matthews, V. M., 125, 130
McIntire, C., 116, 117, 120, 123, 125, 133
McKnight, E. V., 27, 28
McNeill, J. T., 102
Mehta, V., 49, 54, 95
Mitchell, J. J., x, 4
Moltmann, J., 6, 9, 59ff, 66, 67, 69, 97, 99
Montgomery, J. W., 131
Moody, D. L., 103, 107
Moskin, R., 53
Murray, J., 44

Nash, R., 115, 129, 130, 139
Niebuhr, R., 10, 18, 23
Nietzsche, F., 17
Niles, D. T., 24

Ockenga, H. J., 125, 126, 127
Ogden, S., 82, 83
Oosthuizen, G. C., 96, 105
Overbeck, F., 15, 17

Packer. J. I., 114
Pak, C. H., 27
Palmer, E. H., 94
Pannenberg, W., 5, 7, 19, 59, 66ff,
Park, A. P., 59
Park, T. S., 93, 95, 96
Parker, T. H. L., 12, 13
Pittenger, N., 82, 86

Ramm, B., 13, 78, 127ff, 134, 135
Reese, W. L., 84
Reid, W. S., 122, 145
Rendtorff, R., 66
Reymond, R. L., 92
Rhee, J. S., 19, 112, 113
Rian, E. H., 116
Ridderbos, H., 27, 35, 37, 51
Robinson, J. M., 63
Robinson, J. A. T., 7, 9, 33, 46, 47, 49, 50, 53, 55, 56, 57, 58, 87, 89
Roy, R. L., 123
Runia, K., 16, 20, 37, 136, 141, 144
Rust, E., 82, 84
Ryrie, C. C., 109, 110
Ryu, T. S., 36

Sandeen, E. R., 115
Sanderson, J., 137
Scaer, D. P., 59, 63
Schaeffer, F., 4, 13
Schlatter, A., 39
Schleiermacher, F., 10, 104
Schmidt, K. L., 26, 28
Schrotenboer, P., 20
Scofield, C. I., 107, 108
Seerveld, C., 145, 146
Skilton, J. H., 99
Smith, J., 94, 96
Snyder, D. N., 11
Spener, P., 101ff
Stonehouse, N. B., 31, 117, 118, 120
Stott, J. R., 95
Suh, N. D., 74

152

Takenaka, M., 47, 48
Takutaro, T., 18ff
Tavard, G. H., 92
Teilhard de Chardin, P., 75ff,
  83
Tillich, P., 7, 47, 53, 58, 81, 82,
  84, 87ff, 93, 95, 100
Torrance, T. F., 10

Van Buren, P., 49, 60
Van Elderen, B., 30
Van Til, C., ix, x, 1, 3, 7, 10,
  12, 13, 15, 16, 17, 24, 43,
  51, 64, 70, 78, 87, 91, 93,
  100, 101, 128, 129, 134,
  135, 137, 138, 139, 140, 142
Vos, G., 51

Wallace, D. H., 40
Warfield, B. B., 130, 136
Wesley, C., 104
Wesley, J., 102
Westermann, C., 67
Whitcomb, J. C., 137, 138
White, E. G., 94, 96
Whitehead, A. N., 82, 84
Wilckens, U., 66
Williams, D. D., 82, 84, 86
Woodbridge, C., 125, 129
Wright, G. E., 41

Yoshio, N., 27, 87
Young, E. J., 41
Yun, S. B., 36

Zylstra, B., 139

III. Subjects

Adam, 23
American Council of Christian
  Churches, 123
Anabaptism, 95, 96
Apostleship, 31
Atonement, 37, 114
Autonomy, 4, 6ff, 83, 101

Bible, vii, ix, 7, 11, 12, 13, 16,
  20ff, 23, 27, 41, 43, 57, 63,
  70, 87, 90ff, 94ff, 97ff, 100,
  105, 109, 113, 114, 126,
  129ff, 130ff, 135ff, 142, 144
Bible Presbyterian Church, 120
Biblical Seminary, 131
Bob Jones University, 125

Calvinism, viii, 37, 63, 101, 103,
  115, 116, 118, 119, 120,
  129, 134, 135, 141ff
Chalcedon Creed, 24
China, 75
China Inland Mission, 105
Christianity Today, 126
Christomonism, 44
Concordia Seminary, 131
Confucius, viii, 24, 54, 56, 92
"Correlation," 88, 91
Covenant College, 137
Creation, 5, 43, 78, 80, 84

Dallas Theological Seminary,
  133

"Death-of-God" movement, 46,
  59, 81, 83
Demythologization, 5, 33ff, 69,
  141
Dialectic, 13, 16, 64, 67, 69,
  70
Dispensationalism, 106ff, 115,
  118, 119, 120, 121, 125,
  127, 129, 135

Election, 22, 25, 51, 86
Enlightenment, 1ff, 6, 17, 51,
  114
Epistemology, 5
Eschatology, 9, 41ff, 61ff, 63,
  64, 96ff, 99, 127, 135
Eternity, 14, 44ff, 61, 65
Ethics, 12, 53ff, 60ff, 124, 138ff
Evangelism, 49, 102, 103ff
Evolution, 73ff, 114ff, 122ff,
  127ff, 138
Exaltation, 21
Existentialism, 35, 36, 66, 68,
  87
Experience, 12

Faith, 7ff, 25, 35ff, 39, 58, 64,
  67, 68, 71, 88
Form Criticism, 26ff, 40, 43, 87
Free University of Amsterdam,
  142
Freedom, 62, 77, 84
Fuller Seminary, 125, 128

153